Before and Laughter

Carol –
You are such a jewel –
I really treasure our
friendship! Thank you
In all the new ideas you've
given me.
Tous serons toujours amies!
Love,
Sandy

Sandra Moulin

ISBN: 1456509993
ISBN-13: 9781456509996
LCCN: 2011901836

Dear Reader:

After spending 11.5 minutes searching the web for the deep foundations of humor and the burning question, "Why do people laugh, and at what," I have come to some highly valuable conclusions. People laugh for the following reasons:

1. They think that what was said or done was funny.
2. They are nervous and don't know what else to do.
3. They are in a good mood.
4. They are dumb.
5. They don't want to cry.
6. They feel good when they laugh.
7. They are embarrassed for the person who said something that wasn't funny.
8. They are extremely polite.
9. They like to see people who are trying to be funny fail.
10. They are reminded of something else that is funny.

If any or all of these reasons are true, there will be SOMEONE who finds humor in the following pages. Reactions to humor or attempts at it can range from a smirk to a guffaw. Some people will laugh out loud while others won't laugh, but they'll tell someone else that what they read or heard was hilarious. Some people can't find humor in anything. Those individuals should not read this book.

In my humble opinion, laughter and seeing humor in the world around us is an antidote to the pain and tragedy we see and hear everyday. Being able to laugh at ourselves and not take ourselves so seriously keeps us grounded and cheerful. Most of us are funniest when we try NOT to be, but those of us who are always so serious can be comical just for that reason.

It is my hope that you will find something amusing in the following pages, and that it will spark memories of other funny experiences you may have had. One smirk, one laugh-out loud reaction will make my efforts worthwhile. Enjoy.

Any errors in this book are strictly intentional. I am a recovering Perfectionist.

Waiting...

Well, it's December 27, and I am sitting here in the hotel after breakfast waiting for "something to happen" before traipsing down the hall to the Fitness Center (three old machines and too many mirrors) to work out before heading home to experience seven hours in a "Burricane."

I have just finished Norah Ephron's new book, and I realize that I am very jealous of her and other humorists such as Dave Barry, Lewis Black, Bill Cosby and Erma Bombeck. I am jealous because I am an aspiring humorist, and I have no name recognition. I'm just "Fifi." No one has ever heard of me except the 3000 students I inspired (how, I'm not sure) who sat before me in American public schools for 40 years. They thought I was hilarious, but their grade points were indirectly tied to their frequent fits of laughter.

I am NOT a screen writer who has a gift for making the obvious hilarious. I am NOT a man who can make fishing hysterical (and I can't use bad words). I am NOT a political satirist who has a MENSA certificate (in the bottom of his sock drawer) who can make the Bible sound funny, and I am NOT an African-American television personality who can inspire the world with simple phrases like "If you're trying to please everyone, you're bound to fail," or something like that. (I wish someone had told me **that** when I was seven.) I am

NOT a dead housewife who can make the world laugh at lost socks. No, I am NONE of those who have set the standard for bestselling humor tomes.

No, I am just ME, just "Fifi" trying to help the world see the mundane upside down, backwards, in slow motion and 3-D (sans lunettes).

I want people to say, "Isn't she hilarious?" "Where does she come up with these zany ideas?" "You just HAVE to read her latest book." I want Oprah to call me in person and beg me to be on her new show. (I think she has a new show. I'm not sure as I've been busy trying to make dust amusing.)

I want to be famous, but the real truth is, I'M SCARED. I'm scared people will laugh at me. I guess that's a good thing, and, now that I think about it, this is what I'm trying to do: make people laugh. Even if they laugh AT me, they are learning something about themselves—like they are rude, insecure and jealous. Hmmm. . . . Did you hear the one about. . . .

What Makes Me
The Only Person
Capable Of Writing
This Book:

1. I was married almost 20 years to a man who did not talk.
2. I have been married for 18 years to a man who won't stop talking.
3. I crack myself up.
4. I am easily annoyed.
5. I have taught over 3000 teenagers and survived.
6. I speak eight foreign languages, six of which I made up, and one that has no sound.
7. I am multi-talented. I have just not discovered these grand talents yet.
8. I like mincemeat pie.
9. I have been walking on 4-inch stilettos for over five decades.
10. I have the body of a 20-year-old, and the neck of a 90-year-old.

The rest you will discover as you read on.

People Laugh At the Strangest Things

Today I went to a ladies' lecture. I counted at least six times where the ladies laughed when there was absolutely nothing funny. I lay awake nights trying to think of "rolling on the floor" material, and then I find people laughing at nothing.

The lecturer said, "It used to be that you couldn't wear white after Labor Day." Everyone laughed. I see nothing funny in that statement. I leaned over to the woman next to me and said, "Why is everyone laughing?" "Because we all know that you can wear white after Labor Day." That really explained it.

I have come to the conclusion that laughter does not mean that something is funny. Apparently, there is nervous laughter, sympathetic laughter, tragic laughter and, thank goodness, laughter at something funny. I was kind of holding out my laughs for the funny category. Maybe I should give up trying to be funny and just write tragic stories for people to giggle at. I must admit that a few months ago, while watching "The World's Funniest Videos," our whole family was in stitches watching people fall down. These poor fools were falling off trampolines on their heads, falling off bikes on their backs and tripping over fur balls. We were all howling. This is not good.

When reading the funnies, I never crack a smile. Most of it is not clever, cute or even worth a giggle. People LOVE the funnies. I suppose it's just a mirror of ourselves that makes people laugh. Molière and Shakespeare had the idea centuries ago. We still laugh at mistaken identities, lovers hiding under beds when the husband returns, or misers hiding their money in cabbage patches.

With all of the tragedy and sadness in the world, maybe people will laugh at anything just because it's not sad. I took a humorous storytelling workshop years ago, and the premise was that all humor comes out of tragedy. By the end of the five-day workshop, I was sobbing. What's funny about that? Someone recently defined humor as tragedy separated by time and space. Years later, it is rather comical that I ended up sobbing at a humor workshop.

My father was very clever, and he was master of the pun. His was groan humor. My mother wasn't funny, but she always laughed at my father's pathetic jokes. What a good sport she was. I inherited my father's "clever" gene, but I do not tell puns. I do like to make people laugh, however, and I am funniest when I am not trying to be. There are some friends of mine who like to brag about how funny they are. They are not funny, but it's funny that they think they are.

I deliberately try to say dumb things sometimes, especially on the tennis court. I like to see how people react to stupid statements and incorrect score-keeping. It's hilarious how upset people get with me. They have no idea that I am intentionally baiting them. I suppose that's not very Christian, but it brightens my day. When I tell them I'm kidding, they don't believe me; they'd rather think that I'm a dizzy blond.

My husband is hilarious. He does some funny things like making weird faces, pulling his pants up under his armpits like my dad used to, and putting his face right in mine when I wake up in the morning. He is funniest though just because of his personality. He's like Monk—constantly rubbing, scrubbing, straightening, organizing. He gets enraged over unimportant things like the newspaper not arriving by 7:05 a.m. This is all very endearing. The first year we were married, I wanted to strangle him; but now I just use his idiosyncrasies for my writing. Thank goodness he's a wonderful sport.

When I think of who or what makes me laugh, my list is very short. The only program on television I find laugh-aloud funny is *Two and a Half Men*. It's funny that the star of my favorite comedy spends more time in jail than on the set. They should do an episode from his cell. Now that would be funny.

Humor is very personal. If we all laughed at the same things, that would be way too weird and boring. I'm just glad there are poo bags and obsessive-compulsive men because I will always have a reason to chuckle.

I Don't Know

I DON'T KNOW why, but I want to write a novel. I want it to be so riveting that every book club in the country will be clamoring to get a copy, and bookstores will be begging me to hold signings and readings. I don't care if it's the first and last novel I ever write, I just want to write it. I want the descriptive passages to come alive as though the reader had a movie screen in his mind and could visualize every action, reaction and tense moment. I want my writing teachers of the past to contact me and apologize for all the nasty things they said about my writing. I want to hear the applause, feel the adrenaline flow through my veins and imagine my headshot (looking glamorous, of course) on the front cover of *O* and *Cosmo*. I have no idea what this book will be about except that no one would ever have thought of writing such a book, except me. No one has MY imagination, MY experiences, MY perspective, and that's what I love about writing. I don't have to compete with anyone else's style unless I'm trying to win the Nobel Prize, and I'm not.

I believe the impact of my fame will be tenfold since I am old, and people think that once you've hit 65, you're extinct. This is not true. It is in the 60s that there is finally time for reflection and introspection without children running in and out, husbands demanding dinner on the table at 6:31 and committee meetings taking up half your life. Now is the time to CREATE, and I am ready.

But what do I write about? Murder, sex, kidnapping, politics, house-cleaning, our trip to Australia, my flower child loony sister, my dead dog Butch? The categories at the library and the bookstore were labeled centuries ago. I would like to create a NEW category like "Weird Writing" or "Absurd Annals" or "Raw Renderings." These will undoubtedly NOT sell, but it's fun to think about.

They say in my "Learn to Write" books that I should write what I know. At my age, I am finding out all the things I DON'T KNOW! Maybe I should call it "I DON'T KNOW," and start writing from nothing.

OK. Here goes.
Chapter One:
I DON'T KNOW ABOUT BRUSSELS SPROUTS

Chapter Two:
I DON'T KNOW ABOUT TRAPEZE TRAINERS

Chapter Three:
I DON'T KNOW ABOUT INNER TUBES

How am I doing so far? Hmmmm. I DON'T KNOW if this is going to work.

I have already written about body image, retirement, children, grandchildren, husbands, marriage, divorce, vacations, careers, family, friends, traveling, fruit and naps. What else is left?

Students Say The Most Hilarious Things

As I reflect on my fabulous career of 35-plus years as a French and English teacher, I recall fondly many of the hilarious things my students would say and do. Dealing with 14 to 18-year-olds for 108,000 months, I have material for hundreds of stand-up comics. Unfortunately, I am NOT one of them. Much of the humor I witnessed and provoked was of the you-had-to-be-there genre. The facial expressions, the body language, the sound effects all contributed to my holding my gut and rocking on my stilettos listening and watching these kids. I miss so much about teaching, but most of all, I miss watching them grow and listening to their stories and comments through the years. My first class of students is now 62 years old, and my most recent ones are now 23. Many are married with children, some even grandparents. How can this be? Here are some of the unforgettable remarks I will always cherish:

Que diable, madame!
Tu es folle, madame.
Ce n'est pas juste, Fifi!
J'en ai marre, vache!

To this day, I miss the ones who chose to hang out at my desk after school. I loved the ones who chose to confide in me and trust my confidence. I appreciated the Geeks who helped me with all of the audio-visuals and technology which were way beyond my pea brain. I learned from those smarter than I was and from those whose personal lessons touched my life. I laughed at them, with them and because of them. They provided me with a stage of my own creation, and they were my little "stand-ups" that I could not be myself. With the invention of Facebook, I can now watch many of their lives evolve, and I feel blessed to have played a small role in their history. I know they will be thrilled to purchase one of my fabulous books as well as to pass the word on to all of their friends, relatives and Facebook buddies so their French teacher will become rich and famous, and they can say "C'était, Fifi, la folle, mon prof de français!"

What I Learned From My Foo (Family Of Origin)

From my mother:

1. Always look your best (you never know who you will see at the beauty shop).
2. Don't wear your heart on your sleeve. (go sleeveless)
3. Be sure your purse and accessories match your outfit.
4. Stand erect (find a guy to be and do the same).
5. LIGHTEN UP! (My mother had no tolerance for self-pity)
6. Drink at least two martinis before dinner.
7. Brag about your legs. (I don't do this, and she shouldn't have)
8. Always have your own stash. (she kept hers in a gold change purse)
9. "Keep a little mystery about you." (She kept her love affairs secret)
10. Be sure to nurture your female friendships, as women will always be there for you.

From my father:

1. All boys want to get into your pants.
2. No guy really LOVES you—it's a means to an end (no pun intended)
3. Don't spin your wheels (I still hate this one)
4. Think of every experience as a way to grow.
5. Get busy.
6. Never think about being bored; there is way too much to learn.
7. No success comes without hard work.
8. Practice, Practice, Practice.
9. Don't settle for being secretary when you can be president.
10. Don't spend time alone; it's bad for your mental and emotional health.
11. Don't do anything without getting paid for it.
12. If you're going to be a golfer, you must be the club pro (He never saw me putt)
13. Look it up. (He'd never tell me things, even if he knew)
14. There's lots to do between kissing and intercourse (He never divulged this information, and I'm still trying to figure it out. Did he mean play golf?)

What chance does anyone have when parents brainwash us?

Regifting

The other night at my GNO (Girls Night Out) dinner, one of my dear friends regifted me. She gave me a couple of darling bath fingertip towels that said on them, "Who needs men when you have Cosmos?" I thought they were very cute when I bought them for **her** being that she is single, and I'm not. I had dropped them off at her store for her birthday in August and told her young employee to tell her Happy Birthday from me. Either she never got the message or forgot I had given them to her, but I got them back for Christmas. I never told her, but it did make me chuckle. The whole idea of regifting is humorous and dangerous.

I have regifted good bottles of wine occasionally, but that's it. Even then, I felt somewhat guilty, even though they had been unopened, and I am not drinking much wine these days. (After the towels, I turned to Cosmos!)

When giving some thought to the whole concept, however, I've come to the conclusion that there are things we could and should regift. Here are a few that came immediately to mind at this time of year:

compassion
apologies
love

patience
kindness
silence
compliments
laughter
humility
unconditional love

I told my daughter in an e-mail tonight that the best gift I could give her is unconditional love. I was not brought up with that luxury, even though my parents meant well. There are things I wish my daughters would do and not do, but I love them no matter what. Now that they are mothers, they know how challenging it is to love unconditionally, especially when children defy us, lie to our faces and make unrealistic demands on our patience and time. Loving them unconditionally will become a legacy, and that is the best Christmas gift or REGIFT I can imagine.

Do You Remember Your First...

cupcake, Chuckle, jump rope, Slinky, Toasted Almond, box of Crayolas, small carton of milk, marshmallow peep, movie newsreel, Cracker Jack prize, pair of Keds, love note, spelling bee, date? What scents, textures, emotions do these evoke?

Will our children look back after 50 years and reminisce about their first iPod, burrito, blog, GPS, download, CD burner, mosh pit, pair of UGGs, text message, cargo pants, bikini, tattoo, piercing, Facebook friend?

2011: Do you wonder like I do what's in store for us in this New Year? Will asparagus be in? Will the iPhone become an overnight relic? Will high tops be worn with tuxes and lipstick shades turn purple? Will mega-mansions be out and 1000-square foot patio homes be the norm? Will there only be ONE bank, ONE department store and ONE gas station? Will a machine fill up your tank while you're ordering your groceries online? Will someone invent a sport that will instantly decrease bad cholesterol without medication? When we think back to all of the astounding inventions and changes over the past ten years, who can imagine what the future will bring? Hopefully, it will usher in positive change and improved lifestyles.

How times have changed. In each generation, a new culture evolves. The younger one would like to believe his or hers is better, more intelligent, more creative.

The truth is, however, that trends will wax and wane, but we will not be defined by them; we will embrace them, let them go, and watch a new generation create its own. Historians will catalogue them, while philosophers will reflect on the absurdity of it all.

My First Sexual Experience

"Oh, my gosh. What have we done, Bill?"

"What do you mean, what have we done?"

"My father would kill me if he knew you . . . touched me."

"Your father has warped your sense of reason. He thinks all sex is dirty."

"I know, but I think it is."

"How can it be dirty when it feels so good?"

"He said, you'd tell me anything to get me to do what you want. Is that true? Is that the only reason you say you love me?"

"Oh, good grief! Of course not. I can't believe how he has brainwashed you. We haven't even done anything yet."

"You'd better go. I have to think about this."

"Don, you are like a brother to me. I have to tell you what just happened. Can you come over right now?"

"Sure, Ann. I'll be right over. Are you all right?"

"No, yes, well, I'm not sure."

"Who's home?"

"No one. My parents are at the club and Bill just left."

"Thanks so much for coming, Don. I can't believe what just happened. I need you to be my friend and tell me what to do."

"No problem. It must be bad. You're on the verge of tears."

"He touched me."

"What do you mean, he touched you? Where?"

"Right here on my sissy blouse. He touched me more than once."

"I did that to my girlfriend too. I have been feeling pretty guilty about it myself."

"Do you think I've ruined the relationship? Do you think he'll respect me still? My Dad says once a guy does something to you, you will no longer be a conquest, and he'll dump you."

"I don't think that's necessarily true, Ann."

"I hope not. I would just die if he didn't like me anymore.

"You'd think that by 28, we'd have a better handle on this," Don said.

Determined, Driven, Disciplined And Disenchanted

When I think about my goals and aspirations, I get very tired. I AM driven and determined to accomplish many tasks on a daily basis, but I often wear myself out with all my self-imposed discipline. Thus, disenchanted, I head straight to my pillow and blankie.

Each day, I cheerfully embrace the 12 hours before me eagerly approaching my list of "to do"s with energy and enthusiasm. Here are a few things I regularly expect of myself:

1. make bed (placing pillows perfectly on bedspread)
2. workout for 25-30 minutes with weights and weight bar
3. write at least 2-4 award-winning humorous essays that will surely make me famous
4. straighten house
5. make phone calls
6. read e-mails and respond
7. read
8. do errands
9. play tennis

10. think
11. organize cleaning and entertaining schedules
12. read paper
13. check "Care" list and send cards or buy gifts for those in need
14. prepare dinner (at least once a week)
15. take nap
16. drink eight full glasses of water

It's not just the "to do" list that is demanding; it's the "DO NOT DO" list as well:
1. do not eat sugar
2. do not eat fat
3. do not drink
4. do not waste time
5. do not annoy husband
6. do not snack
7. do not worry
8. do not envy women who have house cleaners
9. do not be jealous of other women who don't have wrinkles
10. do not think about friends with perfect skin
11. do not covet my friends' enormous diamonds
12. do not look back with regret
13. do not feel guilty that I don't live close to our grandchildren
14. do not feel guilty that I don't cook very well (he is still begging for tuna-noodle casserole)
15. do not feel guilty that I still haven't cleaned out my makeup cupboard (after 5 years)
16. do not forget to sign up for Yoga

This makes 32 things in which my pea-brain is engaged on a daily basis. No wonder, I am mentally exhausted by 2:00 p.m. If I spent 20 minutes on each of these endeavors, that would total 640 minutes of the 720 available to me. This is all very overwhelming. I need another nap.

Memory

How do we know when the memory starts to go? I forget. Oh, yes, here are a few questions to help you determine where you are in the line-up of forgetful fools.

1. How many times have you lost something in the past three days?
2. How many movies have you rented that you've already seen?
3. How many books have you bought that you've already read?
4. How many names have you forgotten this week?
5. How many times have you left something somewhere this week?
6. How many times have you asked someone the same question this week?
7. How many times have you walked into a room only to forget why you were in there?
8. How many phone calls did you forget to make this week?
9. How many times did you remember your recycle bags this week?
10. How many times have you asked a question and forgotten the answer?

I forget why I wrote this.

HDLLDLWhat the "L"?

Wouldn't it be amusing for seniors over 70 and young people under 30 to switch rides? Picture a 78-year-old bald-headed, pot-bellied geezer cruising through Sonic in a canary-colored Mustang convertible with his radio blaring Lady Gaga. Behind him creeps a 22-year-old surfer dude smoking a pipe in his beige Town Car with "Blue Moon" wafting through the French fry fumes.

Geezer screeches to a stop, removes his backward ball cap and his headphones, pulls his blue-jeaned, barefooted leg up onto his seat and greets the Sonic skater-chick.

The 28-year-old maneuvers his pride and joy into the small parking spot, removes his tweed newsboy cap and driving gloves, dons his readers and clears his throat. The waitress skates up to the window of the Mustang and clenches her giggles between her Envisilined teeth. Geezer orders a Super Berry Shake and a large order of onion rings.

He asks, "What do you do after work?"
She gasps, "I'm babysitting for my grandpa who thinks he's 16."

Skater girl approaches the Town Car trying to camouflage her smirk. "Blue Moon" looks up and asks, "Do you have any meat loaf and mashed potatoes?"

"No sir," she manages, "we just have burgers and dogs."
"Oh. I'll have a burger well-done with horseradish and a side of catsup. You can hold the fries—cholesterol, you know."
"And to drink, sir?"
"White milk will be sufficient."

Skater girl races back into the shop. "You aren't going to believe this one!"

In the meantime, Geezer looks over at Surfer Dude and says, "Nice ride. When I am your age, I hope I can afford slick wheels like that."

Surfer Dude smiles politely. "It was my birthday gift from my gastro-enterologist. He couldn't believe my numbers last visit."
A half hour later, the two finish eating simultaneously, and they both pull out of the drive-in. Geezer revs his canary, and Surfer Dude yells out the window," Let's see what you've got there, old man!"
The two pull up next to each other at the light and Town Car shoots four car-lengths ahead. Stunned, Geezer shrugs, turns up Lady Gaga, pulls his ball cap down and heads for the batting cages.

NOTE:
For those of you who are too young to understand HDL and LDL, these are tests that rate your cholesterol levels to determine whether you are eating too much bad stuff. If you eat too much fat, your arteries will get clogged, and you will croak. I read this on the Internet.

I Wish I Were a Kid

When I look around at restaurants and stores at little kids, I wish I could do what they do. They crawl around on the tables, under their chairs, lie on the floor with a binky in their mouths and fall asleep wherever they want. They stare into space and don't answer whoever talks to them, and they sit there while their parents serve them and clean up after them.

Kids can whine, throw tantrums, wipe their noses on their sleeves and burp aloud, and people think they're cute. They can single-handedly take over a restaurant and cause all the customers to flee, leaving the space empty so they can sing or scream.

Kids don't have to pay the bills or worry about the budget. They don't have to dress themselves, put on make-up or shave their legs. Kids can get praise by simply not talking or sleeping. I would love just once for someone to say to me, "You look so cute under that table." The last time I remember being under a table, I had a bottle in my hand, and it didn't have a nipple.

Kids can completely lose themselves in fantasy and ignore their surroundings. They play the roles of various characters, disguising their voices. I love listening to them play the role of their parents while talking to their dolls or their little robots. They scold and they threaten to put them in "time out." As an adult, I would die to have a "time out." Just lock me in a quiet room and tell me not to come out until I can behave myself. I'd stay in there for a week.

Kids can say all the "inappropriate" adult words and claim not to realize what they're saying. I think a bunch of six-year-olds meet in the cellar (where I used to play doctor) and discuss how they're each going to say bad words to see what the adults do. Parents hear these words (always pronounced loudly in front their friends), and they get all flustered, apologizing, "I don't know where on earth she got that word." Hah. Guess Mommy better stop saying the "b" word around little ones.

Kids get to earn prizes and money when asked to perform routine tasks like picking up poo in the yard or collecting pine cones for the centerpiece. I would like to earn a new pair of Manolo Blahniks. I'd scrub the garage floor, change the oil in the cars or iron his boxers for one itsy bitsy pair of MBs.

Kids get to go to bed after story time usually before 9:00 p.m. I want someone to read some stories to me, tuck me in, and tell me "sweet dreams." If I get to bed before midnight and don't wake up with nightmares about drinking under some table, I'm ecstatic.

Kids get to color. I used to love to color. Do I have my own fat Crayolas? No, I do not. Do I have my very own packet of wide-lined paper with wood chips in the lines? No, I do not. Do I get to go out of the lines like little kids? Of course not. It's so unfair NOT being a kid.

The last time someone asked me what I wanted to be when I grew up, I was 37. My oldest daughter figured out by the age of 12 what she wanted to do with her life. She told me cheerfully, "I want to work at NOT being YOU."

Revelations

I thought a "lift" was an elevator.

I never thought I'd order from the kiddie menu at Cracker Barrel. Ten years ago, I would have worn a mask there!

Sometime during the night, an ATV got into my bed and ran over my neck.

My senior discount now provides me with .50 off my groceries IF I arrive between six and six ten a.m. dressed in chartreuse carrying my own grocery bag. Tuesdays only.

Calcium sucks.

I won't be old until I purposely get on a tour bus.

"Ah, you don't work anymore?" (bitch)

I hate my elbows.

Now that I'm mainlining Vitamin D, I have a sunny disposition.

They say at my age, we have "senior moments." I'll be darned if I can remember any!

Male noises are multiplying.

Remember when "cholesterol" was just a word in the second grade spelling bee?

Don't eye doctors know we memorized the eye chart in third grade?!

My face would look great if I could just walk horizontally.

"RETIRED" = tired and then tired again. Only the reasons have changed.

In my next life, I'll have dimples in my other cheeks!

Who Am I?

Poem:
    Medicare, menopause, men are dumb
    Cholesterol, calcium and Extra Strength Tums
    Whitening, bronzing, it never ends
    Botox, Restylane, not yet Depends
    A whole new list of words to know
    Ones I never knew years ago.
    So sad.

Things I don't want to hear:
"at your age..."
"after menopause..."
"some middle-aged women just..."

" I don't have any of those spots yet."

"Good morning, ma'am. Do you have a senior card with us?"

AARP, SHMARP!

Now that we've moved south, I understand the "no see-ums" issue. I can't see a damn thing!

Since I retired, I've only worn three outfits.

I have no intention of visiting any doctor with an "ist" at the end of his title.

I miss my buttocks.

The only problem with being the breadwinner is you have to pay for all the bread!

What's "social" about "security"? We can't afford the pig roast!

Now that he has his own tux, and I have a collection of lovely gowns, we can no longer afford the "black tie" events. We will wear them as costumes in October.

How can I be old enough to have cataracts? The doctor must get a kickback on eye patches!

I exfoliated 74 times before my dermatologist appointment.

White teeth are over-rated.

I went to my personal trainer today. He is twelve.

Pleasing a man is passé!

What chance did I have? My role models were The Breck Girl, Marilyn Monroe and Lucille Ball.

I wonder if Howdy Doody ever remarried?

Braces at 60? What am I thinking?

My friend says there are three things a woman needs when she retires: her own computer, her own bathroom and her own car. I disagree. The only thing a woman needs when she retires is her own money and a good pair of earplugs.

I've learned how to punish him. Hide his remote, his glasses and his toolbox.

Attention all thirty to fifty year-olds: take numerous pictures of your necks. Frame them. Wear gaudy necklaces to draw attention to the neck. Enough said.

I don't know what this says about me, but I find Paul Newman, Clint Eastwood and Lassie irresistible.

The only cures I ever hope to want are mani and pedi.

Our waiter was so outstanding the other night, we gave him an 8.3% tip!

How many of your women friends do you really LIKE despite their beauty, their intelligence, their creativity, their compassion, their sincerity, their talent, their gorgeous husbands and mansion-sized homes?

Are you creative? Talented? Intellectual? Beautiful? Kind? Charitable? Rich? Employed? Then I hate you.

When I said, "You aren't the boss of me!" He hid my nasal spray.

My floss got stuck in my molar last night. And I told him, I came to this marriage with no strings attached.

I need to see my esthetician. I've been walking around with unibrow for two months.

Be honest. Did you EVER pick your nose?

I hear there's pot at the end of the rainbow. Cool Man!

This morning's paper says that "floods" are out. Why didn't someone say something?

I prefer novels replete with sex and violence. Plot is optional.

Funny, I haven't been invited to join the book club.

Women are vicious, catty, vindictive, and bossy. Everyone knows it all started with the Moanin' Lisa.

Sometimes when I am feeling particularly vengeful, I will order him a Pink Squirrel!

Eight of my nails always look perfect.

I always know just what to wear. Someday society will accept it.

Since when did they design floss undergarments?

Tonight we ate in front of the television for the first time. When we eat in front of the radio, I'll worry.

Whoever said that looking your age was a mortal sin, anyway?!

I've decided it would be cheaper to have my remaining skin dyed to match my liver spots.

We have a consultation next week with a new doctor. We were told to bring all the bottles of medication we are presently taking. We have to hire a U-Haul.

Who decided to make a calcium pill the size of a polish sausage?!

I'll be right back.

How is it that every bad thing that happens to him is somehow my fault? I'm sending him back to his cave.

It used to be that if I lost him in the store, I just stopped to listen for his animal noises. Lately, however, there is an entire chorus of them. Ladies, we are saints!

I thought that once we retired, we'd be all relaxed. No schedules. No rules. No responsibilities. What was I thinking?

He thinks my kitchen is a California Closet. I haven't seen my mixing bowls for months.

Are we laughing yet?

Things I need to learn before I'm REALLY considered old:
1. Learn how to record programs on the digital HD television.
2. Learn how to pay all bills online.
3. Learn how to text message with my thumbs.
4. Learn how to talk on my cell phone, order a Diet Coke at a drive-through and change into my bathing suit—all at the same time.
5. Read a map.
6. Remember all my pin numbers for the correct accounts.
7. Give up trying to be young.

Song Titles:
1. Fairy Tales Suck
2. Cry Me A Vodka
3. Show Me The Way to Leave Home
4. All Alone And Feeling
5. You Ain' Nothin' But a Senior
6. Johnny, Be Bad!

My greatest fear is public humiliation. My second greatest fear is forgetting where I put my Sour Patch stash.

Hold your heads up high, ladies! Never give up, no, never give up your youth! Hang onto it for dear life. Remember, no one can make you feel old, but you.

Quotes From The Queen

1. Do not approach the throne while the QUEEN is on it.

2. There should only be ONE cook in the kitchen, and it should never be me.

3. Children should not be seen or heard unless I am in a very good mood.

4. Husbands should agree with everything the QUEEN says and does.

5. Politics are for little boys in sandboxes.

6. Women should be seen and heard.

7. Men should have to carry a woman's purse for a day.

8. Men should pump gas, not pass it.

9. Women should mow the lawn, and men should make ratatouille.

10. Men should have to play a sport for ten years before being allowed to watch it on television.

11. All teenagers should come with warning labels.

12. People over 80 and under 40 should not be allowed to drive.

13. Life is like bad cheese. You just never know when it's going to stink.

14. Life is good as long as there is wine.

15. Children are the punishment for unsafe sex.

16. Shopping is the cure for dysfunctional marriages.

17. My stilettos have become passive aggressive.

18. My toes are going the wrong way.

19. Familiarity breeds children.

20. QUEENS don't bake. That's why Sara Lee was born.

The Age Test

If you are OLD, you own the following.

1.   a curling iron
2.   a shower cap
3.   a bathing cap
4.   baby powder
5.   heels taller than one inch
6.   skirts longer than mid-thigh
7.   unpatterned pantyhose
8.   Retinae

If you are OLD, you eat the following:

1.   fiber
2.   protein
3.   fruit
4.   whole wheat toast
5.   oatmeal
6.   salmon
7.   York paddies

If you fail the AGE TEST, you are OLD if you care.

46

Sex And Lingerie

When I was preparing my trousseau a hundred years ago, I recall thinking deeply about what to buy to wear to bed. At that time, the soft flowing chiffon lingerie was popular, and what young twenty-something could resist looking like a lingerie ad. My mother bought me my first white nightgown with a matching coverup, and I was so thrilled. I wore it once for about 24 seconds, and after that, it sat in my drawer for months. I remember correcting papers in it years later and counting the ballpoint pen marks.

After a few years of marriage, I moved from Stage I: Chiffon to Stage II: Flannel. It was cold in the winters, and I didn't need to sleep with the nubs. The flannel was not plaid, however, but the short nightshirt was warm, and didn't get wrapped around my calves. (In those days, we didn't have matching panties that said "Good" and "Night" on each cheek.)

After 15 years, I resorted back to the lingerie mode to put some additional spark into our sex life. By this time, the styles were more prostitute-like with bustiers and garter belts. What sane woman would go to bed in a bustier? The stays would not stay, and neither did I. The "Baby Doll" look was also "In." This consisted of a piece of material tied in the front that barely covered one's upper body, and a pair of panties that couldn't cover a mouse. Comfort was obviously NOT part of the designer's criteria. I found that returning in our convertible to the place we used to park as teens was a better spark-producer. (We did get caught by the police, but as my husband was an attorney, they let us go.)

I tried sleeping in my birthday suit, but I woke up without gifts, so I said "Forget this."

It has been over 30 years since all of this angst over bed attire, and now I just enjoy sleeping through the night. We never have sex in bed anyway, so I have saved a lot of money to buy Edy's Caramel Delight.

What Is Victoria's Secret?

It doesn't take a rocket scientist to figure this one out. The secret is that 12-year-olds have taken over the marketing for this former sophisticated lingerie resource. Yes, 12-year-olds. Some may be thankful that these pre-pubescents aren't sitting in front of a video game or hiding in the back of some 17-year-old's Blu-ray, flat-screen television-equipped Silverado.

But, come on. Twelve years old? Some of them appear to have had some "work" done or else they have genes we'd all die for. As a woman of a certain age, I am sad that these girls have jumped from childhood to pre-Hollywood without enjoying the awkward pre-teen stage. As for the rest of us women who might like to buy something sexy, looking at the styles on 12-year-old Brittany-esque models is very disconcerting. The only way we can think about making a purchase is to get out our yearbook photos and paste our faces onto the "Angel" ad.

There are now several different ways to enhance our double As. We can go the "Very Sexy" route with those exact words plastered on our silk cheeks, or we can choose the "Body by Victoria" style, a more conservative way to hoist the sisters into view. I don't know about YOUR sisters, but mine need all the hoisting they can get. Now for some who need a miracle, there is the now almost old-fashioned "Miracle Bra" line. This style takes the lift to a whole new level. I wonder if men can tell that a woman wearing one of these puppies is more foam than flesh. Just hug her, and there's your answer.

The Victoria Secret catalogue has turned into a pre-porno-Playboy magazine. Whoever is teaching these 12-year-olds how to pose has succeeded in creating a miracle. They look like they're 30 years old (an innocent-looking 30-year-old). Replicating burlesque dance moves in still photos is a whole new concept. I couldn't look that enticing without an air brush the size of a palm tree.

The prices of the lingerie modeled in the catalogue are rather steep. A typical bra starts at around $48 without tax. I'm not sure if that includes the gel insert. With a piece of silk fabric the size of a shoe-lace (the panty), the outfit would run close to $100. You had best have a very scrutinizing husband or lover to pay these prices. If my friends would buy these tiny pieces (and why would they?), they would never be seen. Under sweats or flannel pajamas, they would go unnoticed.

There are so many styles from which to choose, one would need to lay out each bra in a row and study each one's features. This row of "tata" covers would stretch from one end of a three-story mall to the other. There is the "demi," the "full coverage," the "no-visible lines," and the 13-way strap puppy. Thinking this much about some-thing to cover 1/100 of one's body is just weird. Can you imagine men looking at 24 different styles of jockey shorts or boxers?

Then there are the panties. The question of the day is just how much of our private parts do we care to expose. There's the high rise, the low rise, the string bikini, the hip hugger, the grandma brief (I don't think they even sell these), or people can just opt for the commando look. (If you don't know what that is, you ARE a grandma.)

I saw something on television the other night where in China, women are wearing skirts with tight-cheeked back views of underwear on them. It looks like you can see their underwear right through their skirts, but it's really the skirt itself! This is ingenious. What warped man came up with the "let's see the tush" design on the OUTSIDE of women's clothes? The cool part is that you can choose the tush you want—tight, round and firm. What will they think of next?

Victoria fans look forward to the billion-dollar diamond-studded bra every Christmas. What woman in her right mind would buy, much less wear a brassiere that costs hundreds of thousands of dollars? The sisters don't know the difference between cotton and carats. The whole idea is ludicrous. (Not that I would take it back if someone were to give it to me, mind you.)

I have tried standing in front of my mirror (in my dimly-lit closet) and copy some of the poses of these teenyboppers. I have the stances and expressions down perfectly: lips just a little pouty, hip thrown out to one side, stilettos poised to confront and hair flowing blond and sensuous down my back. The only problem is my crepey thighs, my sagging jowls and the cellulite at the base of my buttocks. Other than that, I look damned sexy!

Thanks, Victoria, for sharing your secret.

Following The Rules

Isn't it ironic that we spend at least half of our lives bemoaning the rules we must follow only to discover that we have become **rule followers** as adults. In school, annoying bells reminded us to get out of liplock to get to class on time. When we learned to drive, we had to stay in the lines and push the lever to signal our turn (well, some of us learned that). When we got jobs, we had to pay taxes and fill out forms correctly. When we went to stores, we had to stand in lines and wait our turn. When we joined the country club, we had to wear certain clothes on the golf and tennis courts. (no sexy tank tops or short shorts with raggy seams) When we played sports, we had to obey the rules or people would throw clubs or rackets at us. There is no end to rules, and now instead of ignoring the rules or deliberately breaking them, we have become THE RULE POLICE.

At the beach, people are supposed to keep their dogs on leashes. Many don't. It makes me so upset. They don't even carry poo bags. Dogs run here and there, and owners smile as though their kid was taking his first step. I just want to hold up a sign that reads, "CAN'T YOU READ THE RULES?"

Driving down the main drag of our town, people don't use their signals, they weave in and out of traffic, and some just stop dead in front of you. It's absurd, not to mention dangerous. They speed, they use both feet to brake, and they read the paper, put on their make-up and talk to their CPAs while driving. I just want to hold up a sign that says, "DO YOU HAVE A DRIVER'S LICENSE?"

Grocery shopping is no exception. People sneeze on the avocados, burp on the asparagus and walk right in front of you while you're looking for the Chicken Noodle soup. They don't even say "excuse me." They reach right in front of you, run their carts over your flip flops and take the last roll of toilet tissue. I just want to hold up a sign that says, "WERE YOU BROUGHT UP IN NEW YORK?"

There are many unspoken, unwritten rules that people have not learned. For example, when a husband takes his wife out for dinner, she should always have the "good seat." He should pull her chair out for her and smile as she looks over the sea. Then he should be cheerful and romantic while facing the brick wall.

When a husband buys a holiday gift for his wife, he should never buy her practical gifts like scales, irons, string trimmers or falsies. If he insists on this behavior, the sign she would put up would be X-rated.

Wives must also follow certain unwritten rules. When a man is reading the paper in front of the football game, she should refrain from asking him how he feels about changing the wallpaper in the powder room. When the man is locked in his cave, she should not listen to her newest rap disc while practicing her tap dancing.

Rebelling against the rules is a rite of passage for young people. Following the rules as adults is pathetic.

Straighteners And Slackers

Some people make the bed every morning; others don't bother. Some take a stab at making the bed by tossing the pillows where their heads were. Some smooth out the sheets as though they had to balance a glass of red wine on them. These people painstakingly craft French corners and smooth the bedspread several times to be sure there are NO wrinkles. They take great pride in arranging decorative pillows on top of the sleep pillows.

Why do some people make their beds and others don't? Some people are still rebelling at their upbringing where "everything had a place..." Some people feel compelled to make the bed because it gives them a sense of control over their lives. Some only straighten things that others will see (spouses and children don't count).

Straighteners and slackers wander among us daily. Look at any group of people and try to guess which ones make their beds and which ones don't. Are straighteners Type"A"s and Slackers lazy? With whom would you rather be in a hurricane? With which ones would you prefer to travel?

I am a Straightener. I admit it. Worse yet, I am married to a Straightener. As a recovering Perfectionist, I have tried to leave the bed unmade, really tried. If it's not made 20 minutes after breakfast, he's in there cussing at all the pillows and pulling the bedspread over the unsmoothed, un-French-cornered sheets.

Then there are those who feel that the sheets must be washed every 48 hours. These people might be Straighteners or Slackers. There is no logic here. They apparently use their sheets differently than most, or perhaps they are obsessed by the latest bed bug scare. Their 600 threads are now down to about 74.

Straighteners and Slackers who sleep with others of the same or opposite category have other issues about which to be concerned. SLEEPING together. The first decision to be made when beginning the sleep pattern of a lifetime is who sleeps on which side. I know which side I sleep on at home, but I do not necessarily transfer this information to Hampton Inns or Ritz Carltons. He does. If for some unknown reason, I lift my weary core onto the "wrong" side of the bed, he quickly reminds me that it's "HIS" side. (I have trouble figuring out my opponent's backhand, especially the lefties, but that's another story)."What difference does it make," I ask annoyed."You KNOW I always sleep on THIS side," he scolds. I don't go there.

Once into the "right" side of the bed, there's the age-old challenge of SLEEPING with this person. I have tried drawing an imaginary line down the center of the bed. Absurd. I have tried short-sheeting the bed to punish him when he rolls over on me more than seven times, but that only caused more issues. I have tried tapping, smacking, moaning, singing, whistling. Nothing works. His side is the entire bed.

If I'm lucky, I get a few good winks between thrashes. Then there's the noise factor.

No human noise ever sounded like what comes out of this man's nose. Sometimes it's like a distant train whistle. Often it's like being on a hog farm. Occasionally, I will think that we are finally getting the thunderstorm we've so badly needed. If it's a busy night, these sounds will often be accompanied by short moans, loud sighs or intermittent coughs. The worst part is that the sounds never come out at a steady pace. Just when I sleep in between the sounds, he changes the rhythm. Then he will be very quiet, and I will just have fallen asleep when the cacophony resumes. All these are on a good night.

He says, "When I snore, just gently tap me on the shoulder and tell me I'm snoring." Does the absurdity of what he's saying register in his "right" mind? Once I have been awakened to tap him gently, I am AWAKE. This does not help my problem. Hello.

I am happy to report that I have found two solutions to this problem. First, I bought a noise maker. Putting this up to the loudest volume once he's on his train, I can focus on the waves, the stream, the white noise to fall asleep. This works for me 98% of the time, and I am much more rested and less likely to hide his underwear.

The second solution is to get up, once I'm awakened, and go upstairs to write ridiculous little pieces like this one. I have my breakfast at two, three or four o'clock in the morning, and then return to bed the minute he's out of it. It's like double cheating. I get my work done while the rest of the world is fighting the "sleep with your partner" battle, and I get to sleep in the big bed on EITHER side for as long as I wish. Now if it isn't obvious, I am retired, so I have few commitments before 9:00 a.m. One of the greatest joys of being a retiree is to treat oneself to a nap. My nap is very precious to me for obvious reasons.

I lay down on the floor next to the bed, put a small towel under my face, pull my throw over me, turn on the white noise, read for less than four minutes and fall into a deep coma. No pillow, no sheet, no partner. Ah, life is good.

P.S. For those who work, I understand, as I had a 35-year career which forced me to be up and moving at 4:30 a.m. In those days, I took naps with a 15-year-old black fur ball with green eyes whose purring became my 4:00 p.m. lullaby. I used to wake up with something that felt like wet sandpaper tickling my nose. As for my night partner, I just slapped him silly!

Living With Another Person In The 21st Century

The Big Guy may have created us, but I don't think He put a lot of thought into two humans living together for more than enough time to create offspring (however long that may take—another subject). Living together fifty years ago is much different than cohabitating in the age of Technology.

There are certain guidelines that should be met so that spouses do not murder each other. Actually, if you ever wanted to feel as though you wanted to murder someone, living together would be a good apprenticeship. Here are some guidelines I have set forth for posterity. This is not to imply that they are followed, but in a perfect world (21st century only) it would look like this:

Chores: Man does all.

Remote: Woman has total control.

Social Plans: Woman in charge.

Outdoor Maintenance: Man only.

Repairs: Man only.

Finances: Man supplies funds, woman spends.

Parenting: Man relieves woman whenever asked.

Groceries: Woman's job.

Sex: Up to Big Guy.

Conflicts: Man owns shit.

Investments: Man supplies money. Hires expert.

Technology: Each spouse has a computer, iPod. iPhone. Man fixes wife's if not working.

Vacations: Man supplies funds. Woman plans trip. Couple enjoys.

Credit cards: Man supplies funds. Woman spends.

Schlepping: Man's job.

Errands: Woman makes list. Man does.

Compatibility: Man compliments woman frequently and sincerely. Woman tells him he's hot.

Garbage: Couple makes. Man disposes.

Movies: Woman decides. Man goes. Man pays for Junior Mints.

Sports: Man plays with men. Woman plays with women. Man plays with woman when invited.

Compromise: Man gives 75%.

Alcohol: Man buys. Woman drinks.

Cooking: Woman cooks when in the mood. Man smiles.

Romance: Man sets stage, woos wife. Wife decides if she has a headache.

Newspaper: Man shares front page with woman and doesn't spread entire section all over breakfast table.

Idiosyncracies: Man apologizes often.

For Men Only

One would think that by the 21st century, men would have some clue as to how women tick. The problem is that women don't tick. Men tick. They are like clocks—steady, predictable, deliberate and balanced. Women, au contraire, are UNpredictable, random, excitable. They are beautiful bundles of raw energy and emotion. Why would a clock marry a clock? Clocks like reasons to keep time, and women are their "raison d'être."

Men need to understand that women don't necessarily say what they mean. Women expect men to draw conclusions, make assumptions, and use their right brains to glean meaning. This is extremely challenging to the clock. He is just ticking along his merry way trying to keep order. Women and men have different definitions of "order."

For men, "order" means the "usual," the "predictable." For women, "order" means putting all the unpredictables in a logical arrangement in order to deal with them four at a time.

Men logically tackle one task. When they complete that task, they begin another. Women, out of necessity as mothers and household managers, learn early on to multi-task. Ask any woman to engage in a discussion while she's doing the laundry, unloading the dishwasher, baking the bread and listening to her Spanish vocabulary on her iPod, and she'll gladly agree. Ask a man to do that, and he would look at her like she was an alien.

The trick to marital harmony is for each sex to understand the unique workings of the other. One would think that agreeing to their differences in genetic and biological make-up, couples would rarely fight. The divorce rate says otherwise. The only logical explanation, therefore, is that one or the other of the sexes doesn't "get it," OR one or the other of the sexes is trying to change the unchangeable. It's just that simple. Ask my attorney.

I Love Men

I LOVE MEN. I don't pretend to understand the way they think (assuming they do), but I do really like them. I don't know if they are the stronger sex, but I know sex is strong with them. I don't know if they're smarter and less emotional than women, but I really don't care. I want my man to be smart, and less emotional than me, but I don't want to deal with his emotions, and I don't want to compare his brain to mine. We don't have similar brains, and that's what makes relationships so wonderful and so frustrating.

Men are tall boys. They are simple and literal. If you ask them a question, they will answer it. If you tell them something private, they will keep it that way. If you expect to understand their motivation for dumb comments and insensitive behavior, forget it. They usually don't know the sources themselves.

Men like cars and trucks. Men like sports and stocks. Men like sex, beer, motor oil and fish. How could any woman expect a man to understand why he said something or didn't do something with that kind of mentality? Men don't have reasons behind their behaviors; they make up the reasons only after they've been confronted. Men don't like conflict, but they'll argue to be right as if their last brew depended on it.

I have no problem with men who want to be right as long as I am not wrong. I have no problem with men who watch Sunday night football as long as I have my own TV. I have no issue with men wanting sex as long as it's not during my soap or my nap.

We women need men. Without them, imagine how our lives would be different. Who would mow the lawn, take out the garbage, carry in the groceries, change the oil in the car, make dents in the leather couch, wake us up in the middle of the night, clean the garage, spread the mulch, take the holiday decorations down from the attic, talk to the guy in India, spread fertilizer, put up the Christmas tree, spray the shrubs and discover the blue food in the refrigerator? Who would ask the obvious? Who would ask the same question ten minutes later? No, men are special. They are hopelessly endearing and eternally annoying, but I love them.

The Perfect Man

If you could take Steven Covey, George Carlin, Abraham Lincoln, George Clooney and Marcel Marceau and put them all together, imagine what you'd have! The PERFECT MAN. Take the organizational skills of Covey, the sense of humor of Carlin, the integrity of Lincoln, the drop-dead gorgeous looks of Clooney, and the instant-silence talent of Marceau and VOILA: there he is.

Every woman would like to have a man with his nose pointed "True North." This man, Covey, knows himself well. He knows how to organize his life. He is an expert at prioritizing. He understands "urgent" versus "put-it-off," and he has the "right" values tattooed in his heart. How does this translate for women? Simple. "True North" means he's always focused—he doesn't look around the room when you're talking or thumb the remote while you're kissing his neck. He is organized. This means he picks up his clothes, keeps his drawers and closet neat, remembers to pick up the cleaning and fill your tank and cleans the fridge when the food's about to turn blue and fuzzy. His priorities are in the right place: YOU ARE THE QUEEN AND YOU COME FIRST. He understands that "urgent" means "do what I ask you to" NOW and that "put-it-off" means there are serious consequences. The "right" values are pampering the little woman, taking the little woman on fancy trips and treating her to only the finest in gourmet cuisine. Covey is the man!

George Carlin's universal sense of humor was priceless (rest his soul). In case the man of the family forgets, an entire library of Carlin's books and tapes are displayed openly on the bookshelf. Carlin told it like it was and is. He knew how to make you laugh at the mundane, and his lens on society's behavior made us all look at ourselves less seriously. Husbands who listen to and read this humorist's genius will always realize that the George sense of humor can diffuse an argument, lure a woman to bed and offend his mother-in-law so she'll leave the house.

Abe Lincoln was a man of integrity. It wasn't his fault that he was gunned down while attending a play. (Now that I think about it, maybe that's why men don't want to go to the theatre.) Integrity is an admirable character trait, and it translates into husbands always telling the truth. For example, when a wife says, "Will you hang the picture of my mother over the couch within the next hour?" he will answer, "Yes, sweetheart." This does not mean that he won't mutter every George word in the book while begging the neighbor to take his hammer into his house and hide it. He can then say HONESTLY, "Honey, you know, I can't find my hammer."

George Clooney, ECFTS (Eye-Candy-for-the Soul), is every woman's dreamboat. Our Perfect Man will have his looks, his money and his charisma without his reluctance to commit. He will dazzle her friends, but like Abe, never hit on them. He will tell Carlin jokes without the vulgarities, and he will honestly admit that he thinks his wife is beautiful in front of her jealous girlfriends.

Marcel Marceau is dead. This is very sad, as a quieter and humbler soul there never was. This man mimed his life away. Our Perfect

Man would go into the mime zone whenever the wife gave him "the look." He would never one-up her, step on her in conversation, contradict her when her hyperbole was out of control and would always smile silently.

This Perfect Man needs a woman. Which woman? YOU!

Let It Fly!

When mothers raise little boys, they must teach them to let everything go—spiders, frogs and gas. I have never understood why girls' mothers teach the exact opposite. Little girls grow up with their faces all scrunched together trying to "hold it," while little boys just giggle and let it fly. They even have contests to see who can "toot" the loudest. If girls do it, it's vulgar and "unladylike;" if boys do it, it's funny. This must be the foundation of the double standard.

Little girls are given books like "Cinderella," "Sally Goes Shopping Alone," and "Beauty and the Beast." Little boys are given books like "The Gas We Pass." Little girls dream of handsome men carrying them off on white horses and beasts turning into Brad Pitts while little boys are learning to gross out little girls.

Little girls are brought up to be beautiful, ladylike and polite. No respectable young lady would ever make animal noises in public. No honorable young woman would bring attention to herself by spreading a caustic odor throughout an enclosed space. No intelligent young woman would stand next to someone and let him know what she had for dinner. Boys—just the opposite.

It's bad enough that men feel entitled to share their bodily functions with the world, but public places such as highways, bookstores and cocktail parties should be off limits. What mother would purposely teach or allow such behavior? If that's how she wanted them to operate, she should have taken them back to the cave.

As young girls begin to mature, they learn to admire their bodies and perfume them. As young boys begin to mature, they learn to play with their parts. This playful activity never ceases. What do men find so fascinating about this? Some little boys even like to announce their bodily functions in public.

Our four-year-old grandson's latest plaint is, "Mommy, my wiener is tight!" My daughter, mortified, tells him to think about something else. Little boys somehow learn to read certain magazines to ease this tension.

Somehow men feel that this biological entitlement also implies a right to do or say anything they choose whenever and wherever. The "right to be right" syndrome is evident at birth. The "let it go" lesson above translates into male conflict resolution in relationships. Men just "let it fly" and "let it go." They tell us we're making mountains out of molehills because we don't understand the "let it fly" or "right to be right" mentality. And to think it all started with a fart!

Hiding Places

When I think about what is valuable to me or what I want to hide from whomever, I think about places no one would look. First, what do I have to hide? (that I can put in writing)

Sometimes I have a "private stash" that I hide from my husband. This is truly absurd, as he really doesn't care if I hide my money. He doesn't want or need it, but it makes it more fun to hide it anyway in case he should change his mind. He is "of a certain age" so who knows when this may happen?

Secondly, I have letters and poetry I have written that I would die if anyone ever saw. I don't want to throw it away, and when I reread it, it makes me realize that I'm not as insane as I was when I wrote it.

Finally, I have photos of former loves (some vintage 1960!) that I can't bring myself to throw away. If something happened to me, I wouldn't want my daughters to think I've been cheating on their father. Besides these men are probably all in a home by now.

So the question remains: where do I hide these valuables?

I took an inventory of the house yesterday, going from one room to the next to find creative corners for hiding. Here is a list of my findings:

1. Tape to top side of ceiling fan. (This would require dusting first so the tape would stick.)
2. Tuck into pocket of 1950s pedal pushers.
3. Slide behind photo of our dog (1949).
4. Tape to inside of Bundt pan never used.
5. Hide in Bisquick box on pantry shelf (the one that says, expiration June, 1974)
6. Tape to bottom of fruitcake.
7. Stick inside my father's diary from 1944.
8. Attach to bottom of couch. (This would require dusting first so spiders would not eat the stash)
9. Hide in safety deposit box in the next county.
10. Set on top of husbands "Honey, do" list. He'll never look there!

The Budget

The word budget should be erased from the English language. It raises blood pressure, causes marital distress, disrupts sleep and cramps creative shopping.

My husband and I never had a budget until we retired. This was not a planned event. In fact, we both dreaded the thought of having to control our spending. With no income other than our social security and our pensions, we had no choice, however, so this is my interpretation of how our budget works.

All monies are put into a pot. The Queen (that's moi) pays certain bills and the prince pays the rest. Whatever is left over after each one pays the bills is theirs. Mine comes out to about $900/month, and his is around $4.26. I am fair, though, as I only make him fill the tank once a week.

The budget is divided into categories: HOUSE (mortgage, groceries, utilities, etc.), CARS (insurance, gas, etc.), TAXES, GIFTS and CHARITIES, ENTERTAINMENT AND **THE QUEEN'S WARDROBE (QW).**

As I pay for the groceries, I decide what and how much we consume. I am always careful to budget my grocery spending very carefully so as to have plenty of cash left over at the end of the shopping. This surplus stash goes directly into the QW coffee can for special purchases and sales.

The GIFT category is also the Queen's responsibility. I make sure to comparison shop, gathering numerous coupons along the way so that there will be money left over from the budget. This money will also be added to the QW coffer.

Entertainment includes meals out, entertaining friends, and attending concerts and plays. I am also in charge of this category. Meals out are tough, as I like NOT having to cook (it's a Queen's prerogative). Entertaining friends is a little easier to manage, as I can always ask each guest to bring something very expensive, while I supply the lettuce and butter. Concerts and plays are harder to manage, as the prices are usually fixed. By asking friends to drive, this saves on my gas budget, so I can squeeze a few $20s out of that category.

Another trick I use is to offer to return any purchase the prince makes. This way I get cash, and because he forgets to ask for it, I stash that too. My QW is one of the best in our hamlet.

The budget isn't really that bad. I just don't like the word. QWS would be preferable—Queen's Wardrobe Stash.

Form Xmkspt

This test is for women who are considering tying the knot after having been married at least once. These questions will clarify any misconceptions they may have about their future spouse.

1. How many times have you been married?
   a) one
   b) three times
   c) five times
   d) too many times to count

2. Do you have any of the following life-threatening illnesses?
   a) heart disease
   b) cancer
   c) emphysema
   d) split personality disorder

3. Do you believe you're right
   a) all the time
   b) some of the time
   c) most of the time
   d) Why would I answer this?

4. Do you consider yourself affectionate and romantic?
   a) yes
   b) no
   c) When I feel like it.

5. Do you have any children under 40?
    a) yes
    b) no
    c) not sure

6. Do you have all your parts?
    a) yes
    b) no
    c) not sure

7. Do you have health insurance?
    a) yes
    b) no
    c) sometimes

8. Would you sign a pre-nup?
    a) yes
    b) no
    c) sometimes

9. Do you have any pets?
    a) yes
    b) no
    c) sometimes

10. Do you like fish?
    a) yes
    b) no
    c) I prefer Canasta.

Dearest Wife 1:

I hate to bring this up, but after ten years of marriage, I am really tired of mowing the lawn, trimming the hedges, emptying the garbage, walking the dog, cleaning the garage, washing the cars and putting up the Christmas tree. I know you have many responsibilities too, but I am ready to relinquish mine and have you take over. I will gladly take responsibility for cleaning the junk drawer and making the bed. In this day of women's equal rights, I am certain that your taking over the above chores will empower you and make the ladies at your Bridge Club admire you.

P.S. Have I told you lately that I love you?

From your first husband,
Fred

What Women Don't Understand

There are three things women don't understand: working the remote, driving the sports car and watching the sports channel. Women think men don't hear when they are engaged in these activities. This is not really true. Men pretend not to hear, as there are too many syllables involved to deal with the discussion, and the two words they **would** say would be beeped. Women's mouths go very fast when men are focusing on the field goal. Men do not want to talk about bridge next Saturday with the Shenkels while the clock is running out.

Even though the wife paid off the sports car with her "own money," the man prefers that she NOT drive the sports car. She might back it into something, park it too close to a 4 x 4, shift incorrectly or stall it at a busy intersection. Who knows what could happen. It is for her own safety that she NOT drive it. Women do not understand this. They are full of syllables regarding this issue.

Men like to skip around with the remote to be sure they aren't missing anything. The remote is a control device. It allows the man to be sure there are no weather warnings, no vulgar programs designed to corrupt the little lady and no "explicit" scenes to offend her.

Women do not understand this protective cave-man-type behavior. They indulge in more syllables which just fall on deaf ears.

Speaking of deaf, sometimes men get hearing aids when they hear perfectly. This is a passive-aggressive defense mechanism to keep syllables from crowding the hearing ducts.

If only women understood. There would be more peace in the world.

Men Say The Darndest Things

"Honey, would you get me a beer?"
What, is he crippled?

"Baby, I need an aspirine."
So you don't know where to find it after 20 years?

"Sweetheart, are you going to wear **that**?"
No, I'm just standing here in it five minutes before we leave.

"I'm so tired."
So...

"Babe, did you close the garage door?"
No, I never close it. I figure the robbers will be able to get to my diamonds easier if I leave it open.

"Where are my glasses?"
You must be kidding.

"I have so much to do. I am overwhelmed."

I have nothing to do. I just sit around waiting for you to be UNDERwhelmed.

"I think I'll take a nap."
No reply.

"Could you stop and pick up some sardines for me?"
Sure. After I drop off the recycling, pick up your shirts, gas and wash your car and pick up your shoes from the shoemaker. No problem.

"What did you do today?"
Nothing.

"Did anyone call?"
Only your proctologist.

"Are you going to get the mail?"
No.

Dear John:

I am starting to get really pissed off. I called you over 24 years ago, and I haven't heard a word. You don't write, text, web, nothing. I want you to know that I haven't been sitting around waiting for you. I got married, and we have 10 grandchildren, thankyouverymuch. What about you? What do you have to say for yourself? Are you married? divorced? living in sin? living? How many grandchildren do YOU have? Are you computer literate? Are you text savvy? Talk to me.

When I told you to go home and get divorced, I was just kidding. I was just in a bad mood. Since then, I've been on drugs, and I'm much more even-tempered now, even though, for us, it's too late.

I thought you'd like to know what I'm doing and, more importantly, how I LOOK. I am tall (about three inches taller than when you knew me in '86). I have long blond hair that sometimes hangs across my right eye in a sultry fashion. I have been working with a trainer for some time, so I have significant muscle tone, and my long legs are still drawing looks, even from the 60-year-olds! I wear a big smile 96% of the time, as I'm happy that often. The other 4% is when my husband pisses me off, and then I leave town and charge the spa to him. I am still very sharp mentally, as I can name all 10 of my grandchildren (although I can't remember where they live or how old they are). My friends think I am very funny. I still play the piano like a Van Cliburn wannabe, and I play tennis a lot with those beneath my level. My writing talent has improved greatly, and I'm waiting as I write for my first publishing contract. (I sent in an agent query in 1994). My husband and children still think I'm "cool," so life goes on without incident.

How about you? Do you still have your hair? Are you trim, or is that pot belly thing working its way to you? Do you still smoke cigars? Lord, I hate cigars, but I remember yours smelling pretty good. Maybe it was where you were smoking them. Are you still working? Most people our age retired years ago, but there are some hangers-on. You are probably one of them. How are your kids? Do they still like you? If so, you're one lucky guy.

Where do you live now? We live on the Intracoastal here in the deep south. We love it. Three minutes walk to the pier puts us right on the water where we make out on the wooden bench while watching the sun rise and set. Do you still make out?

Do you still have all your parts? Many people here are having parts replaced. They even have parties that you can only go to if you DON'T have all your parts. I have all mine, thankyouverymuch. So does my husband. That's a very good thing.

Do you still jog? Are you still afraid of insects? Do you still eat Mrs. Fields' chocolate chip cookies? I don't jog or eat cookies, and I was never a ninny to be afraid of bugs to begin with. I squash them in my bare fingers.

Dear John:

I wear a size 0-2. What size do you wear? Is your wife fat? Are you rich? My husband is thin, semi-rich and I'm thin. We belong to a country club where most of the people are much more wealthy than we are, but we're accepted nonetheless. Probably because of my sense of humor.

Well, off to pack now. We're headed for Australia/New Zealand. Do you travel? We like traveling, and I plan to climb the famous Sydney bridge in my 4-inch stilettos. Do you remember them?

You don't have to answer this, obviously. You haven't answered in 24 years, why would you start now?

Yours in friendship,

Sally

Husband Recycling

There should be six huge recycling containers, each the size of a small cruise ship.

The labels would read: MACHO MAN, CONTROL FREAK, MR. RIGHT, BEIGE BUDDY, LOUDMOUTH and TIGHTWAD. In a perfect world of recycling, wives who have had it up to their egos would have the luxury of dumping their husbands into one of these bins and opting to live alone forever or join WOMAN SCOUTING FOR PERFECT MAN.com. (Good luck with that one.)

After being dumped, men in each of these bins are destined to buy personal ads in local newspapers and register themselves online. The ads would read as follows:

MACHO MAN seeks "little woman" to put pot roast on table and warm butt cheeks in lap. Enjoys watching endless hours of sports on television while "little woman" bakes pies in the kitchen. (Kitchen comes equipped with granite counters, top-grade cabinetry and 12 aprons.)

CONTROL FREAK (CF) seeks submissive woman to do as she's told. Enjoys teaching woman to load dishwasher, scour shower stalls and trim hedges. CF allows woman to accompany him to any destination of **his** choice.

MR. RIGHT seeks little woman who is happy to accept blame and admit when wrong. Enjoys winning arguments and seeks someone who likes to spar.

BEIGE BUDDY seeks woman with personality to bring excitement and stimulation to relationship. Enjoys quiet and isolation. Enjoys traveling wherever **she** wants.

LOUDMOUTH seeks woman who listens, laughs at jokes and is hearing challenged.

Enjoys being center of attention and drinking beer.

TIGHTWAD seeks woman who doesn't enjoy shopping, won't turn down air conditioning or turn up heat. Likes women who shop at second-hand stores and save large quantities of money with fists full of coupons.

SINGLE WOMAN AD: Seeks one man who owns his own shit.

"The Look"

With the recent engagement of Prince William, many women look back dreamily at their own engagements. We all remember "the look" our future husbands gave us: a look that said, "You are the most beautiful and wonderful woman in the world." I remember it well, and it made my whole being warm and fuzzy. I have seen this look many times throughout our almost 18 years of marriage, but other looks have also surfaced.

When I tell my Girls Night Out group that I got "the look," it no longer implies love and adoring. It means, "You are embarrassing me again," or "I don't like it when you do that."

My father gave me that look when I was 12, and it is ingrained in my psyche. Anyone since 1955 who has given me that look has had the same impact on me which is a fluttering heart and a mild anxiety attack. The person behind the look could be the guy whose car I just cut off who flipped me the bird or the look of disapproval I used to get from my teenage daughters when I wore something low cut.

"The Look" amongst mature married women is a code for "Wait till I tell you what I did to provoke him this time!" For some husbands, it takes a lot to get them annoyed, while others have a filter that is always on "high alert." My husband is one of these. The behavior that sets his monitor blinking wildly is my having more than one drink, my interrupting him (which I RARELY do), my turning the twist thing on the bread the wrong way and my packing the suitcase inefficiently. He has "his way" of drinking, talking and packing. If you do not follow the "manual" in these areas, you will get "THE LOOK."

Some husbands add the "roll the eyes" thing going along with "THE LOOK." Others add the "look-up-at-the-ceiling-smack-the-forehead-with-the-palm-of-the-hand" reaction. What is truly amusing about all of this is that the woman is just energized and continues to provoke the reaction. What often happens next is that the woman mimics "THE LOOK," and soon both spouses are "LOOKING" at each other ready to pounce. There is an unhealthy dynamic at work here, but apparently we all just "let it go," as we're all still partying and laughing about it.

There is yet another "look," that most women recognize immediately. It's "I'm bored and tired, and I am ready to roll" look. I see it often, especially when my husband drinks. His metabolism tolerates approximately 1/100th of an ounce of alcohol before his entire body shuts down. The other night, I saw the first signs of the above "look," when the "glaze" began to take over, and he answered, "yes" to all questions (except "Will you pay for our friends?"). Once the glaze begins, drool and rubber neck are sure to follow. It is then that the woman must make the ever-perplexing decision as to whether to go home with "excitement boy" or stay and have fun herself prepared for the "lecture" when she returns home. The wife's look of exasperation may be seen frequently at cocktail parties, classical music concerts and shopping sprees.

Ladies, there is one simple way to avoid the "look"—LEAVE HIM AT HOME!

All I Need Is Love

Tennis is not a game for the faint-of-heart. It IS a sport, however, for those who would like to stay in shape and get love at the same time. The score always starts with LOVE, so LOVE is in the air. Once the ball is in the air, however, the love begins to fade, and players start showing their true colors.

My husband who is a 4.0 player (I am a 2.696444) and I were playing doubles with one of his good friends and his wife. His friend is the kind of person you can't help but like as he is funny, smart, an excellent athlete and is interested in others. Once we began our match (couple against couple), however, I saw a side of him I never knew existed. He was out to WIN at all costs. He scolded his wife (also an excellent player) when she didn't do what he thought she should have, and he cursed at himself when he didn't execute as he knew he could. I observed this behavior from across the net, and I thought to myself, "He is going to make mincemeat out of me when we switch partners. Maybe I need to get gas pains or something." He was thrilled when they beat us badly the first set. My husband was already looking gray, and I was trying not to be nervous about being this guy's whipping post.

As it turned out, I played like a 4.0 that day (happens once every 18.3 months), so we won easily, and we are all still friends. I hear he loves Scrabble. I think I'll pass.

It's Never Too Late

When my 70-year-old father found a new girlfriend, Bea, in 1990, I was thrilled. I remember telling all my friends, "It's never too late for love." He was absolutely smitten by this woman, and the two of them spent 20 wonderful years together. They partied, took cruises, partied some more, played golf, ballroom danced and partied some more. When he died two years ago, she was devastated.

Then Bea met Ross, a widower of six years. Their first encounter together after being introduced by mutual friends was to be the most hilarious tale I've heard in months. They had cocktails at the home of the mutual friends. The importance of this detail is that neither of them drinks. After another cocktail each at the Moose (the local dance venue), they danced three times. "He's a lousy dancer," she laughed. I said, "Don't complain; he can stand up." I asked her what he was like. "I don't really remember," she said. I asked what he looked like. "I don't remember that either." "Did he talk?" I asked. "Oh, yes, he talked, but I have no idea what he said." Apparently, he called the mutual friends the next morning to tell them he wasn't sure if he had paid the bill. I can't wait for the next installment of this adventure. At 90.5, it is so refreshing to know that there can still be chemistry and fun, even if one can only remember it for ten minutes!

Ambushed

Just when I'm least expecting it--there it is! I roll down my passenger door window and shout from the bottom of my being with all my might, "HE FAHRTTED! HE FAHHHRRRRRTED!" People out walking their dogs with their poo bags look at me and begin laughing hysterically, falling to the ground, their dogs licking their drooling faces. Squirrels scamper up trees, cats meow, mailmen hide under their trucks. "I can't help it, I'm sick!" he whines. YEAH, RIGHT! OMG! He doesn't think I notice that he's holding his sphincter tight as he holds back his giggles and toots.

Disgusting. What do men find so funny about this? This is the only thing I ever say that my husband finds hilarious. What does that say about my future as a humorist? Must I lower myself to bathroom humor to create a bestseller? Must I spend the rest of our married life being ambushed by caustic gas? The payback is unthinkable.

I am totally defenseless and relegated to spending 24/7 with a handsome, wealthy, intellectual gasbag! HELP!

P.S. He says to me, "You're hilarious!" I say, "What would I do without YOU as my subject matter?" He replies, "NO SHIT!"

Ironing

Women in the 21st century have not heard that IRONING went out with high button shoes. (Actually, the shoes may be coming back.) IRONING is for women (and men, of course) who insist on having creases in pants, perfectly pressed blouses and jackets, and EVEN perfectly flat sheets and pillowcases.

It is my understanding that with the invention of polyester (40 years ago) and no-wrinkle fabrics that ironing is unnecessary. Just think of all the money we would save without having to purchase the board, the cover, the iron, the stuff you put in it (distilled water? or did that go out in the 50s?) and the little trivet to put the iron in. This does not count the time people spend carefully putting the point of that thing into every little armpit and between each button. This is hard on the tennis, baseball and golf arm too.

If a person irons one hour a week at minimum wage (4.73?), that's approximately $20 a month or $240 a year. Someone should be paying you to do this! It's wrong.

Personally, I gave up cotton for Spandex years ago. Some of my friends make fun of my wardrobe, but you will NEVER, I repeat NEVER see me with an iron in my hand. And what about the storage issue? The only reason I would ever consider ironing is the adorable little ironing board cupboards that hang on the wall. They are so cute. It's like playing Holly Hobbie at 60! They should make a tiny iron to put in there too, the size of a pecan sandie.

I will agree that some of my cotton-creased friends look very fresh in their perfectly-pressed attire. The problem with cotton and linen is that once they sit down for more than three seconds or fold one leg over the other, all the wrinkles return so they have wasted all that time at the board.

If someone would iron FOR ME, I would wear cotton, but they would have to come with me wherever I go and touch me up every ten minutes; otherwise, what's the point?

The Junk Drawer

I have to be really really bored to look in, much less CLEAN out the junk drawer. This drawer seems to suck the life out of our house, our pockets, my purses and our tennis bags. The good news is that there is nothing alive or rotting in there, as there is no odor yet.

Here is what I found yesterday while I was looking for a pencil with lead in it:

1. 6 paper clips with fuzz stuck to them
2. 1/ 8 of a piece of birthday wrapping paper
3. a half package of lemon drops all stuck together
4. 9 coupons from 1976 for items we never buy
5. 5 pencils with no lead and no erasers
6. 6 sticky note pads
7. 2 pages of address labels from our previous address
8. a piece of ribbon that isn't long enough to go around any package
9. an empty CD container
10. four empty, but slightly used plastic baggies
11. a roll of toothpicks (bright yellow)
12. one earring and a broken bracelet

I would like to say that there are a few of these items that bring back fond memories, but that would be a lie. I must tell him to clean out that drawer.

God's Junk Drawer

I was just thinking about what the Big Guy might have in His junk drawer. I wonder if the drawer is the size of an engagement ring box or on the order of a cedar chest? We'll go with the latter just for fun.

I am sure He has several letters He has wanted to send to various sinners, but He slept on them (so they're all wrinkled) and decided not to send them. There are probably at least 150 of those puppies in there. Then maybe some well-meaning Martha Stewart types sent Him some recipes that He hasn't gotten around to having His current disciples prepare for Him. So they're all just sitting in there. (the recipes, that is. I don't think the disciples would fit) Such tempting dishes as Sin by Chocolate, Root-a-Beggar Redemption, Caramel Confessions, Pray 4 Me Prune Puree, and Shrimp Soup Salvation would surely please. I imagine He has a lot of coupons in that drawer, like we do. "10% off tithing," "100 Communion napkins for $1, "True Confessions subscription - $2 off," "Bible stories for Boomers at pre-publication rates."

There is undoubtedly a clothes brush in there, as His long robe must get pilled occasionally, and some slightly ripped sticky notes reveal that the Big Guy is thinking of fresh ideas all the time for keeping us all humble.

I often wonder what the Big Guy does up there all day. Does He interface with all the lucky ones who have joined Him up there? Do they all ask for His autograph?

I am curious to know how He feels about technology. I'm sure He must have a computer by now, and, if so, I wonder if He's secretly on Facebook wondering what on earth people are thinking putting so much inane stuff on there. They should all be home praying or doing charitable deeds instead of talking about their sinus infections and their children's potty training.

Does He drive? If so, what kind of car does HE have? Would He have a convertible, an SUV, a sports car? I would imagine it would be something humble like a Buick Century or a used Town Car. Does HE have a driver, and if so, does the driver use a GPS? All of these questions plague me at 3 a.m. when I wake up from my sugar burnoff.

Now I lay me down to sleep, I pray the Lord, my soles to keep. All of these questions are making me tired.

Household Hints

I love household hints. They make my life easier and provide me extra time to bathe in my bubbles. Household hints rule!

Here are a few of mine:

1. Leave hammer and nails on kitchen counter next to framed photograph. Set new Victoria's Secret lingerie next to them.
2. Leave keys to his sports car next to recipe for his favorite casserole.
3. Leave article from newspaper itemizing cost of Holiday Light Hanging companies next to article from *Cosmo*, "Why Women Leave."
4. Set keys to my car on counter next to Car Wash coupons. Place frozen dinner coupons on left.
5. Leave laundry instructions on counter next to a tiny pair of boxers.
6. Leave empty wine bottle on counter next to gas card.
7. Leave toilet bowl cleaner on counter next to disc of "Romantic Music for Lovers."
8. Leave Diners Club bill on counter with zero balance highlighted. Set Victoria's Secret catalogue on right.

9.   Set ad for diamond stud earrings on counter next to con-
     cert tickets for his favorite local musical group.
10. Set travel brochure for African safari on counter next to
     article "Prices Expected to Triple on African Safaris."

Poo Patrol

I like animals. Cats are warm and cuddly, and dogs are smart and loyal. Unfortunately, they all defecate.

When I was growing up, we had pets, but they were kept in our houses or in fenced yards. I was lucky enough to get paid an extra .25 a week to pick up the dog poo in the yard. My father gave me a little shovel and said, "There you go, sweetie." This task did NOT endear me to my pet. I just looked at Butch and sighed, "You are a disgusting little fur ball." Holding my nose, I carried his gift somewhere and disposed of it. I have conveniently forgotten that part. What I never realized, however, is how lucky I was that we had a fenced yard. No one ever saw me carrying around a pile of poo. I would have died of embarrassment.

Times have changed. Many of us no longer have fenced yards, but dogs continue to poo. The result is that highly-respectable doctors, lawyers, CPAs and CEOs amble down the road carrying a variety of poo bags after having stood watching their pet squat and poo in public. I always love to observe the look on the master's face; it's the same as on the pet's. Some owners look the other way so the neighbors can't see the disgusting look on their faces. Others watch as if to protect their pet from sickos like my husband who smashes his smirking face against the car window. I swear that whenever a pet senses my husband's presence, he says to himself, "OK, it's time."

The variety of poo bags is fascinating. Some have a plastic baggy (small 2" x 4" Ziploc). These people are very in-tune with the natural biological functions of animals. They got As in Biology. Others carry a plastic grocery bag so the contents are not visible. The size of the bag is not in direct proportion to the size of the poo. I will not elaborate on this. And then there is the nasty neighbor who just boldly directs his pet to poo wherever, and they both walk away unfazed by the dirty looks we give them at the club.

I would love to have a pet if someone would pay for it, feed it, walk it, pick up its poo and pay for its vet bills. All I would have to do is play with it and hug it. Unfortunately, that isn't how it works. I've considered "rent-a-pet," but I'd still have to do the Poo Patrol.

No thanks. I'll hug my stuffed Benji.

Coupons In The Mail

Every so often an envelope arrives with coupons to save us enough money to take an exciting trip. I was thinking of such glamorous places as Paris, Barcelona, Rome. This is not what the Executive Board of Coupons Anonymous had in mind. What are those morons thinking? Each envelope's offerings become more and more ludicrous. Who is going to cash in on a place where you can have your pet's nails polished for 15% off or where you can have your tires tattooed or your front door monogrammed? Puleeeez!

How about 50% off Ruth's Chris' most expensive steak dinner for two or 75% off a day's kayaking on the Intracoastal?

If they are going to spend postage and kill trees to send offers through the mail, let's have something for everyone. For the texting teen, how about 50% off her parents' phone bill? For the senile senior, how about 60% off of SAM-e? For the busy housewife, how about four house cleanings for the price of one? For the soccer mom, how about free limo service for the kid and his friends for a month? For the shopaholic, how about 50% off all designer handbags at her choice of boutiques? Now THAT would be some savvy marketing.

I am tempted to throw the dumb envelopes out every time they come, as I know I will skip through the shiny slippery coupons cursing under my breath. But, no, I am such an optimist. I keep thinking ONE day they will send me one I can use.

Children Eating Out

There should be a law against children under the age of 30 eating in public restaurants, particularly gourmet restaurants. I am sitting next to three mothers and two children as I write, and I am covered with sippy cup splats and dough balls.

This issue is very controversial, and as a mother of two grown daughters and 10 little grandchildren, I am well aware of the dilemma parents face when they want to take their little ones out to lunch or dinner.

Whenever a toddler sits at the table next to me, I know that the floor will be a disaster once they leave. Fortunately, I don't have to clean up the spilled soda, the gooey bread stuck to the chair legs or the crumbs that cover a 7-foot area around the table. It wouldn't be so bad if the children stayed IN their chairs while creating this mess, but most of them are walking around the restaurant working the crowd dragging their lunch remains with them. They are always very cute, so people talk goo-goo to them, and so they learn that they are cute covered in mustard and catsup. This is not a good message to send to little ones, and the parents are so glad to get rid of them for a few minutes, they just let them go, chanting a very weak, "Come back here, sweetheart. Don't bother the nice people." Hah! They're secretly thinking, "Yeah, bother away. I need some quiet."

We went to a lovely restaurant a couple of weeks ago, and I was looking forward to sitting at a cozy table for four with our friends when I stopped short. There was only one table occupied in the restaurant. At this table was a young couple with a baby who was screaming so loud, I am sure I would have lost my hearing sitting anywhere in the restaurant. We went outside and sat on the patio. When I went back in to the ladies room, there were two tables of young parents with yet another screaming kid, and I thought, "Thank heavens, we didn't sit in there." This has nothing to do with the mess they probably made but everything to do with my hearing and my mental health. The obvious question is, how can the parents enjoy an evening in a lovely restaurant with their kid screaming in their ears? What can be done? Against whom are we discriminating? A retired couple who would like to enjoy an intimate dinner on a Saturday evening or families with screaming kids?

You have to love the irony of it all, however, when due to the poor hearing of our friends, they were talking so loud to us, that we had to move our seats back and subtly peruse the crowd to see if people were bothered by the noise. Maybe people who can't hear well should stay home with the under-30 crowd and turn up the television while slurping their soup off their tray tables.

Robbery

At a cocktail party the other night, the subject of robbery came up. A few people had actually been robbed, so I was all ears to hear their stories. If someone had asked me what I would remove if we were leaving town for a significant amount of time, I would say: cash, jewelry, laptops and my coveted Caramel Delight low-fat ice cream. "No," they said, "That's not what they look for." I was shocked to hear that the most stolen items are drugs (especially pain killers), electronics, sterling silver and piggy banks.

I couldn't believe my ears! They wouldn't want my diamond necklace, my HP laptop that works at least 20% of the time or my whitening strips.

You mean, I didn't have to worry about the $400 I hid in the bedroom before our last trip? The $400 that I hid so well I couldn't find it for a month? I don't have to freeze my father's silver dollars in the stir-fry veggie bag? I don't have to hide my Star Trek pinky ring in the Cheerios box?

What kind of thieves are these guys, anyway? Let me get this straight. These guys are going to sneak into our house, grab my Vitamin C and D, my husband's Viagra, our sterling candle snuffer and my pink piggy bank? What will they do with all that? Take their girlfriends out to a candlelight dinner, counting the minutes until "whoopee" and pay the bill out of a pink hog? That is just wrong.

Topics About Which I Know Absolutely Nothin' (and choose not to)

Cooking

Cleaning

Gardening

Sewing

Crafting

Upholstering

Babysitting

Laundry

Baking

Canning

Knitting

Pruning

I realize this limits the number of men attracted to me. On the other hand, what 80-year-old cares about any of these things anyway?

Everything You've Always Wanted To Know About Fruit

BANANAS are a "clean food." They come dressed for fall and winter, but can easily peel off their outer layers for warmer temperatures. They can be stored for at least three or four days without ripening; however, if they ripen, they can be made into banana nut bread. Bananas can be dipped in peanut butter for a high protein snack, and they can be sliced on cereal for a healthy beginning to the day. Bananas can be eaten in one's hand, as their peel protects the hand from getting yucky.

Bananas have taken on new roles in the last decade. They are now used to demonstrate safe sex by putting a "raincoat" over them in sex education classes. They can be used as telephones when talking to two-year-olds. They can be used as spider hammocks, and one can draw faces on them and use them as fruit dolls. They can also be used as push toys for small pets.

GRAPES are also a "clean food." They don't ever need to be peeled, and their peels keep their juices inside. They can be stored for several days before shriveling up. (It's kind of how I feel after a facial). Grapes can be served as an appetizer for crowds and in fruit salads for dinner guests.

Other creative uses for these small gems could be using them as cover pieces for checkers, and then eating them when the game is over. (green grapes and purple grapes must be used for this purpose). They may be frozen and used as weapons between siblings when parents aren't home. They may be used as earplugs when annoying siblings bicker, and they may be put in the dish with the fake grapes so guests can make fools of themselves trying to decide which ones are real.

ORANGES are also a "clean food." They need to be peeled to eat, but their outer cover is thick and allows them to be used for indoor kickball and catch. They have sections inside which can be eaten one at a time, thus allowing for extended periods of juicy tasting. Oranges may be used for falsies for Halloween costuming and for juggling routines.

PEACHES are not a "clean food." They are too juicy, but they are delicious. They are somewhat fuzzy, and can therefore be used to tickle someone you're out to get. One can make "peach melba" with them. (What is a "melba" anyway?)

GRAPEFRUIT is another "clean food." Grapefruit has its own skin, like an orange, and similarly has sections as well. Grapefruit may also be used for Halloween bust-building and juggling.

PINEAPPLE is sweet and delicious. It comes in a ring form, so when you're bored, just ask your spouse to hold up his "bad" finger, and use the fruit as a ring toss. At the very least, you get him all sticky, and that will be fun in itself. Pineapple may be also be used for large eyes when making a big sheet cake. Use two grapes for the nose and a plum for the mouth. It's sure to be a conversation starter at a birthday for two-year-olds or 70-year-olds.

TOMATOES are fruits, yes they are. Tomatoes are red, and they come on a vine. The vine is green so they are very colorful. Tomatoes are usually used for salads, but they are good weapons for your yearly fight. Take them in the yard, yell obscenities at each other in another language and throw them. It will expel a lot of stress, and watching each other covered with red goo will certainly bring some laughs.

End of fruit story.

Supporting Your Candidate

Recently, I was asked to give a reception for a woman who is running for a non-partisan judgeship. Being the kind fool that I am, I agreed. Rather than having a crowd of people eating and drinking in our modest home, I decided to give a ladies' luncheon. The only problem with this plan is I don't cook, and I hate lunch. Rather than purchasing the food from a nearby restaurant, I determined that this was a perfect time for me to learn to cook. A new quiche pan, brand new individual soup tureens, new fall napkins, napkin rings and ramekins for the chocolate mousse, have already set me back $176.93, and I haven't even bought the ingredients yet. Oh, my.

When I asked the nice lady at the kitchen store about making the quiche crust, she gave me some tips about how to roll out the dough on the pastry sheet. "OMG," I choked. I don't have a rolling pin or a pastry sheet. Maybe I could use one of my husband's old tee-shirts and one of my ten-pound weights instead.

Then there's the issue of what beverage to serve. If I offer wine, that's another $100 plus. If I don't, I am stuck with iced tea (yuck), bottled water (looks awful on the table), diet soda (people will burp and fart), or coffee (stains the carpet and the grout). This all seemed like such a good idea at the time. It's not like this candidate and I are going to be best friends whether she wins or not.

I told my husband that I was going to experiment on HIM for the next several days to be sure that what I serve is tasty. He said under his breath, "Oh, no." The worst that can happen is that I convince myself that cooking is not my thing, and I buy the lunch from the gourmet store up the street. The best that could happen is that I learn to cook, and the candidate hires me to cook for her victory luncheon. Bon Appétit!

The Last Hurrah

My dream vacation is to return to southern France, rent a villa for at least a month and live like a native. I envision myself riding my bike to the local bakery, buying my fresh baguette, bantering with the owner and riding back to the villa to read Le Monde. My husband loves France, and he wants to go with me, but I have given him a condition: he must speak fluent French. Otherwise, my whole plan is ruined. I want to speak the language, live like a resident of the village and travel short distances. He needs to do the same, or I will have only half of my fantasy. The solution: teach him French.

SYLLABUS: WEEK 1

Day 1: Find him.
Day 2: Put a set of earphones and write the French word "paresseux" (lazy) on his desk.
Day 3: Find him.
Day 4: Present the 10-minute a day plan. Explain that the lesson will be daily AFTER he has eaten and BEFORE his nap.
Day 5: Teach first 10-minute lesson. (Wake him up after first 5 minutes.)
Day 6: Work out to relieve stress.
Day 7: Ask him to memorize "La Marseillaise" by next week.

WEEK II

Day 1: Find him.
Day 2: Teach him how to introduce himself, state his nationality (French), and pronounce a list of carefully chosen words (obey, thank you, love, credit card)
Day 3: Review Day 2
Day 4: Teach him how to order from a simple menu. (Tell him he will get this for lunch ONLY if he performs flawlessly.)
Day 5: Give him lunch.
Day 6: Find him.
Day 7: Show video of southern France, and share my "Trip to France" bank statement with him.

WEEK III

Day 1: Review all taught so far.
Day 2: Find him.
Day 3: Teach him how to tell time and explain the 24-hour clock.
Day 4: Review clock, and promise to make him a French dinner.
Day 5: Show him pictures of the villa I have already rented.
Day 6: Find him.
Day 7: Teach him vocabulary to find his way back to the villa.

WEEK IV

Day 1: Review all taught so far.
Day 2: Promise to pay for dinner at our favorite French restaurant if he orders in French.
Day 3: Call therapist.

Day 4: Teach him vocabulary for sending packages back to the States.
Day 5: Teach him how to understand French commands; i.e. take out the garbage, rub my feet, get out of my face, you're doing it again.)
Day 6: Practice commands.
Day 7: Find him.

WEEK V:

Day 1: Call my daughters, and ask them if they want to spend a month in southern France with me.

Guilt

My shrink once told me that guilt is the most wasted emotion. It serves absolutely no purpose other than to take away the enjoyment of the moment. I still have trouble with guilt to this day, and in Pitt Bull years, I am 469. There are numerous reasons for my guilt, none of which is logical or sane. I feel guilty when it's beautiful outside, and I am inside writing stories about guilt. I feel guilty when I'm outside when I SHOULD be inside writing about my guilt. I feel guilty when I eat too much, drink too much, talk too much or think too much. This translates to approximately six hours and 28 minutes per day which adds up to approximately 2292 hours per year or 95 days. This is absurd.

Guilt is just an emotion like hostility, fear, anger, joy and love. Just imagine feeling love 2292 hours per year. That sure would be good for mankind. If I add the hostility and anger to my guilt hours, I apparently have about three good days per year. Oh, my. That makes me feel so guilty!

Who Are You, And Who Let You In Here?

"Don't forget to finish putting the dishes away." (Mr. Should)

"I feel great. I can't wait to get to the computer." (Ms. ToDo)

"I wonder how my precious daughter is faring all alone with four babies." (Mrs. Worry)

"Call Chris to see if her sore throat has gone away." (Ms. ToDo)

"It's another ho-hum gorgeous day in Paradise." (Miss Observer)

"I love it! A whole day to do my thing in an empty house!" (Miss Observer)

"I should call Carol. I feel so guilty I've haven't been over there."(Mr. Should)

"Go online to reserve car and room for trip." (Ms. ToDo)

"The luncheon turned out pretty good, considering I've never entertained 15 people at a time."

"I will work out again today."(Ms. ToDo/Sir Driven)

"I hate the lines in my face." (Mrs. Worry)

"I know I've gained weight. Back to home cooking." (Mrs. Worry/ Sir Driven)

"Only three more days till payday. I don't know how this happens every month." (Mrs. Worry)

Voices, voices and more voices. Where do they come from, and who let them in? Mr. Should, Ms. To Do, Mrs. Worry, Miss Observer, Mr. Nag, Sir Driven. They are all there to greet me every morning at 6:30 a.m. the minute I gingerly lift my body out of bed. They don't wait for me to brush my teeth or wash my face. They are right there staring me in the face--all talking at the same time. I feel like I'm at a sorority reunion.

So what's funny about all these messages that bombard my pea brain as I am trying to ease into my day? Maybe nothing, but now that I am more aware of them and their origins, I understand why I need a nap every afternoon at 4:00. Sleep is the only way the voices will stop--or at least the one way that I don't hear them.

The amusing thing is that we poor souls who are trying to get through our To-Do Lists are fighting crowds of people in our heads--dead, alive or imagined. We are not seven years old with no experience; we are full-grown adults who supposedly learned how to compartmentalize and perform successfully in the work and domestic worlds. If someone were to take a snapshot of any of us suffering from these crowds in our minds, it would be hilarious to see the frustration, confusion, elation, exasperation and jubilation on our faces at any given moment of the day.

Which one is me? Which one are you?

Mr. Should is the most annoying and relentless of all the voices. Mr. Should could be a parent, a teacher, a boss, a child or a disciple from above. Perfection is never enough for Mr. Should, and his list has no end. He is constantly shoulding, peppering us with guilt when we don't obey.

Ms. To-Do might be a mother, a grandmother, a tyrannical music teacher, a pastor or a nun. She has a high-pitched whiny voice that grates on the nerves. She repeats herself and says the same things in different words so you don't even realize she has said the same things 28 times. Her list is never the same as our list, and her standards of completion are unattainable.

Mrs. Worry is anyone who ever scared you as a child. "If you make that face, it will freeze like that." "If you don't watch out, the boogie man will get you." "If you don't clean your plate, children will starve in China." Mrs. Worry loves to fill our heads with useless threats and fears so that while we're trying to heed the counsel of all the other voices, we doubt ourselves every step of the way.

Miss Observer is the camera in our heads. Some people observe everything at once; others observe one insignificant thing for no special reason. Some people who become obsessed with observing (the ADHD folk) cannot focus so they become agitated and unproductive.

Mr. Nag is NOT a woman. Men think that it's only women who nag. This is not true. Naggers know no sex (maybe this is why they nag!) They want things done within seconds of their requests, and when this does not happen, they repeat, often more loudly. Some go so far as to leave tiny sticky notes around the house or cut articles from the paper and lay them on their spouse's pillow. Some repeat the request in six-year-old language to be sure the message is understood. Mr. Nag becomes a voice as well as a whole person, so now you have twins railing at you!

Sir Driven is that voice of ambition and opportunity that some demented parent, teacher or preacher planted in our psyches to tell us to go and do good, to attain our full potential, to reach for the moon. I hate whoever that was, as I am in the driver's seat, and sometimes I just want to coast! Sometimes I'm low on gas, and I want to just rip out the accelerator and drag my feet on the street!

What voices do you hear? If you hear none, you're either dead or asleep.

Hobbies

I am always fascinated by the various interests of others. Some are voracious readers; others are Triathlon addicts. Still others are couch potatoes, and their opposites, avid bridge or chess players. We all gravitate to activities which interest us and to people with whom we share such interests.

I have a group of female friends who fascinate me. They are all talented, creative women who enjoy building, rebuilding, repairing or engineering various pieces of furniture. Some of the furniture is very old; other pieces are sentimental. Regardless, these women do not choose to call John's upholstery down the street and spend $50 to have their possession done by a professional. They would rather get in a car together, visit at least six or seven different cushion shops to find just the right size and shape buttocks holder to cover. Once they have found the framework of their masterpiece, they celebrate by squealing, hugging each other, and talking on the phone about it for hours. The next step is to choose a new fabric to go with the decor. Another trip in the car to at least four or five stores will result in just the "perfect" pattern with the correct "repeat" to begin their project. (So far, they have spent at least $46.00 on gas, $34 on lunch, and four hours on the phone). Once they have purchased the fabric (for half price, of course), they begin to discuss the actual labor to follow. This is usually done around a lunch table with sketches and drawings. Happy with their plan, they return home to the precious possession and begin the work. At least five or six trips back and forth between houses as well as three or four phone conversations later, they have torn apart the old and put together the new. This now calls for a "viewing." Several like-minded friends are invited to the "viewing," where generous servings of wine and cheese are devoured. ($50). Guests "oo" and "ahh", volume escalates, and husbands flee. One hundred thirty dollars and three hours later, the husband returns to a sink full of dirty wine glasses and the stench of warm cheese. He looks down at the "creation," sits down on it, and it rips.

The Women's Restroom

There are some things people need to know about the "Women's Restroom." First of all, it is blatantly obvious that NO WOMAN designed such a place, and I have never seen a woman REST in these places. No woman would design a facility where women must pee, wash our hands, put on make-up, clean our contact lenses, floss our teeth, change our babies, or take pills with less than 25 stalls. It is hard to believe that there are actually restaurants in our hometown with only ONE count'em ONE stall or a ONESIE. I love one of these, in particular, which has a full length mirror so you can watch yourself pee!

Secondly, MEN obviously design these places, as after we wash our hands, the paper toweling is ABOVE the sink. This means that the water and residual soap is running down your arms and into your armpits while you're quickly trying to dry your hands.

And then there is the Handicapped stall. It is not always labeled. I went in one of those today (no label), and it was as big as our master bedroom with its own sink. No handicapped people were around, so I snuck into it while no one was watching. I tried to be very quiet, so no one would know I was in there. (Like they couldn't see my stilettos under the door!) I stayed in there for a long time, just in case someone came in and threatened to report me to the Stall Police.

Men are obviously much less modest than women, as there are big cracks between the stall doors. Little kids love to push their faces up against them and peak in at the worst times. The mirrors are usually opposite the cracks, so people washing their hands can even see in. The male designers must sit around a huge mahogany table in the executive offices and chuckle about what they can do to humiliate women. They must hate their mothers and sisters.

Then there is the baby changing table. Just what I want to see after a full platter of French toast and sausage. I love the old ladies who stand over the mother while she's changing the diaper. They look down and say, "Isn't that the cutest thing?" (I assume they are talking about the baby.)

Trying to wash one's hands with a huge purse over one's shoulder is a major challenge. There is no shelf on which to set your purse, and the counter is always sopping wet, so you can't put a Coach or Louis Vuitton on it. This leaves placing it on the dirty floor or trying to juggle it on your shoulder while washing your hands and combing your hair. Once I tried juggling a huge purse while applying lipstick and the tube went right up my left nostril.

And then there's the listening issue. It seems to me that restaurants should pipe music into the restrooms so we don't have to listen to other not-so-melodious sounds. In one restaurant, there is a recording teaching you how to say "pee" in Italian. It's lots of fun, and it makes the time go fast.

Let's hear it for female restroom designers. They will put a minimum of 25 stalls in every public facility, include a separate restroom for mothers and babies, hang a nice shelf for purses and packages and put a crown on the biggest stall. That one is for me—the QUEEN of innovative ideas for women.

Getting There

My husband and I are preparing to take a once-in-a-lifetime adventure tour of Australia and New Zealand. Other than being sentenced to 40 hours in a giant pressurized cigar tube with hundreds of germ-carrying, loud-mouthed travelers, we are truly looking forward to this experience.

People have given us all kinds of advice about how to survive the flight. Taking drugs and drinking seem to be at the top of the list. That's fine as long as one has no reaction to either, but we are somewhat reluctant to paralyze our brains and bodies for fear they might stay like that (like the expression my mother said would freeze on my face). I heard of one man who took a sleeping pill he'd never taken before. He became disoriented and climbed into the lap of a curvaceous blond across the aisle. He had a wonderful trip, but his wife divorced him, and he's now in a home.

Alcohol can always take the edge off anxiety and boredom. The unfortunate thing about it is that it wears off, and sometimes the result is worse than the cause. I have had a lot of luck with alcohol myself, but the Lilliputian restrooms on the planes are too cramped to chance it.

On long flights, they choose films to ease the pain. We have had such luck as seeing Shrek II, Cinderella, Pulp Fiction and Rocky XII on previous flights. I can hardly wait.

We are only allowed to bring one carry on and two suitcases for this three-week journey. That won't even begin to accommodate my shoes. I told him he has to take less underwear and socks so I can fit my stilettos into the corners. As the weather will be varied in each venue, I need to have clothes for several different climates and functions. A gown for the Sydney Opera, cocktail dresses for gourmet dining, hiking boots for extreme summits are all a must.

The layout of the seats is crucial in surviving this flight. I asked the tour company, and they indicated that it would probably be a 3-4-3 configuration. Neither of these will work for me. Sitting in the middle would be instant suicide. His sitting in the middle would be worse. So it looks like we will have to do the book-end thing. I'm sure the inner two people won't mind if we hold hands over their laps occasionally. (His arms are unusually long.)

The next issue is figuring out how NOT to talk to those sitting on either side of me. The one across the aisle is usually not a problem, but the one next to me could be. I have learned various techniques through the years such as wearing headphones, wearing sunglasses, speaking a foreign language to them if they approach me and just telling them I have strep throat and can't talk. Short of that, I have considered wearing a "don't give me your germs" mask. That usually spooks people.

By the time we get to our destination, all of my creative energy and polite behavior will have been sucked dry trying to survive the flight, so I will need to go to bed for three days before beginning the tour.

I can't wait to climb the 300 story (or is it foot) bridge in my new Michael Kors sandals. My friends dared me, so I have no choice. The trick will be to balance myself and take a photo of my feet looking down through the swinging bridge. My husband is afraid of heights, so I will be on my own.

I wonder if we will take a kangaroo ride to the Outback. Hopefully, my Chanel bag will fit in his pouch. What an adventure this will be.

Time To Leaf

Ladies and Gentlemen:

I would like to thank you all for being here to wish lettuce a fond farewell. After centuries of fiber-filled fun, lettuce has decided to leave us. I realize that some of you will not be sorry to see lettuce venture into the unknown because you are tired of chewing and flossing. Lettuce, after being torn apart, chopped, shredded, stuffed and spun has had enough. Being dumped on by everything from Thousand Island to Garlic Expressions, lettuce is wilted and tired.

Lettuce found it was hard being green and tossed around for years and years. Never really feeling appreciated for being just as it was, lettuce will be happy not to be surrounded by radishes, onions, cucumbers, carrots, celery, and a few nuts thrown in occasionally. When people started adding goat cheese to the mix, lettuce could barely stand the smell. Being housed in a plastic box or bag day after day got very confining, and lettuce felt very alone. It is time for lettuce to leaf!

Dreams

Dreams are fascinating. I wish someone other than Freud had a more amusing take on what they mean. As I know of no one who's done this, it's up to me.

My husband has dreamed of Confederate Cats (life-sized felines dressed up in uniform), and I have dreamed of being married to both of my husbands at the same time. I don't know which is more of a nightmare.

Research from "The Dreams Foundation" (a random article on the Internet whose validity remains unchallenged) claims that "nightmares provide a natural 'pressure release' therapy for the psyche." This means that when my husband dreams of Confederate cats, he is letting his hair down, or something.

It has been said that many artists and musicians have been inspired by dreams. Such well-known figures as Mozart, Beethoven, Stravinsky, the Beatles and Billy Joel have all found inspiration in their sleep. This means there is hope for my creative juices to turn out something incredible. Jack Nicklaus ostensibly improved his golf game by ten strokes through his dreams. I wonder if my overhead could pick up pace if I take my racket to bed.

Have you ever awakened in the middle of the night certain that what you were dreaming about was happening right then? Have you ever gotten up "on the wrong side of the bed" and wondered if it was something you dreamed that put you in a foul mood? Dreams can be very powerful. For example, the other night, I dreamed that I would return to France and live in a villa on the Mediterranean. The next day, my husband tried to French kiss me. Quelle coincidence!!

According to dream theories, if we go to bed with the intention of learning about or realizing our dreams, we may be able to make them come true. I have decided to give myself a target dream for each of the next three nights and see what happens. Night one: having an affair with George Clooney. Night two: Winning a $10,000 shoe spree at Bloomingdales, and Night three: Finding that my husband has hired a cleaning lady for the next year. Night Night.

Male Mall Shoppers

I am always amused when I go shopping (I shop alone) and see the many men sitting outside the stores on benches staring into space. Their wives are in the stores doing some kind of damage, and these men have the "OMG, what is she buying now?" look on their pale faces. These men are usually over 60, which tells me that younger men are either stuck at home with the kids, or they've been smart enough to escape to the nearest Sports Bar while their wives drag the little brats around the mall in their double-wide strollers. I pride myself on being smart enough to have NEVER taken my kids shopping without loading the stroller with raisin boxes, coloring books, animal crackers and brand new pop-up books. I never WANTED my husband to go with me, as it would have been just another kid to entertain—a kid with a calculator built into his brain.

Last night, my husband wanted to take me shopping to buy me a new sexy jacket to wear for "Date Night." (He's 70.) He had a specific image in his mind of what he wanted this jacket to look like. I have never seen him so excited about shopping with me. After about 20 minutes with no purchase, I thought "He's probably getting tired and bored." He wasn't. He was so eager to find just the right jacket that we ended up spending TWO hours at the mall. Watching me try on jacket after jacket at store after store, he was still raring to go five minutes before the mall closed. I could not believe it. We had finally given up and were on our way out when we came upon a store that we had missed. We decided to give it one last shop. Of course, we found the perfect jacket three minutes before the store closed, and it was on sale. I thought he was going to call Calvin Klein himself to share in his glee. We both left the mall all energized as the old bench men shuffled through the doors, their shoulders hunched over and their eyes glazed carrying huge shopping bags. The wives were grinning, babbling about the beautiful holiday lights and exclaiming how much money they saved. My husband was hugging me and talking about what I would NOT wear under my new jacket. Duh. Now I get it.

Dear Mr. President:

There is NO WAY I would ever want your job. You must be so tired. I cannot imagine all the stress and worry there is in your life. You need some FUNNY. I am just the person to provide it for you. You may wonder who I am to so boldly suggest that MY FUNNY will bring you calm and peace. Well, I am NO ONE. Remember Joe, the Plumber? I am Fifi, the FUNNY. Yup, that's me. Fifi. Doesn't that name just bring a smile to your lips? No? Well, that won't stop me. I will persevere. I am tenacious, gracious, loquacious and witty. I am clever and silly and when that doesn't work, I just make faces.

Mr. President, I would like to offer some suggestions to help you with some of the nation's major issues. First, unemployment. There are many people without jobs. This is a bad thing. Have you considered instead of trying to create more jobs, how about getting rid of some people? If there were less people, then the percentage of unemployment would decrease, your approval ratings would increase, and you would have a giant smile on your face. What to do with the people? That's something you need to think about.

Mr. President, the case of immigration is an ongoing thorn in your side. Why not just send a percentage of Americans to other countries (all those born on November 4, 1976, for example) and have them become citizens there, and then the percentage of immigrants would decrease, your approval ratings would soar, and a fresh smile would surface on your face.

Mr. President, the issue of the economy looms large for all of us. There is just not enough money--it's that simple. So you need to tell the Treasury Guys to make some more. You could dole it out like the Black Friday retail sale. Let's say from 3 a.m. to 4:30 a.m., people could arrive with their credit scorecards, and anyone with a Credit Rating of over 850 could pick up a couple hundred. They could then go buy some stuff and rejuvenate the economy. You would be a hero, and you might even utter a giggle (in private, of course).

Mr. President, as a senior citizen who has been down the pike, I am very concerned about bullying in our country. Children are getting beaten up, beaten down and humiliated in cyber space. What can be done? Here's a concept: how about the politicians stop bullying each other all over the media?!! What happened to the days when we revered our political leaders (like you, of course)? Children watch television, and they see movies where people insult each other, swear at each other, beat and cheat each other. Why are we surprised that kids gang up on one another then? Duh.

What can you do? Get rid of the two-party system, and let Americans vote for people of integrity who do what they say they're going to do. What a refreshing thought.

Mr. President, I must close now, as I have more creative humorous thinking to do. I do this best when I am choking down the free breakfast at our travel hotel. Just looking at the breakfast buffet with its cardboard biscuits, plastic food-looking scrambled eggs, green

Dear Mr. President:

bananas and yesterday's gravy is enough to send me into hysteria. I hope your White House breakfast is better than this. If not, it's no wonder politicians get so surly and vengeful. They just need some nourishment!

Yours with all due respect,

Fifi, la folle

Silly "S"

My favorite word begins with an "s." It is not a nice word. It expresses my deepest sentiments about many things and issues. It cannot be replaced by any lame word such as "stuff," "crap," "junk," or "you know what." The "s" word connotes not just a despicable odor but an unresolvable solution, horrific pain, mass confusion and idiotic explanations. My father always told me that people who used such words were just showing their ignorance and lack of class. This may have been true in the 40s, but many words have come into popular usage in the past 60 years that many deem much more vulgar and rude than the "s" word.

We all know "S" happens. Explain this expression to a foreigner. If they learned the meaning of this term, they would be very confused. They would think you were talking about bodily functions. This is far from the truth, especially if you're constipated.

This expression means that something happened that displeased you to the point that exclaiming, "Oh, darn!" doesn't cut it. "I am unhappy about this situation" doesn't even come close, and no gesture conveys the humorous aspect of this cry.

George Carlin used to say, "It's all Bull "s—" I don't really agree with him totally, although I must admit that much of "it" is. It's like the ants that dragged the dung up the hill and cried, "This "s" has gone far enough."

Some people who don't believe in "s" say, "No, s." I don't believe that either, as I think there is much "s" around, and that's no "s."

After this piece, I could apply for the bleeper on television that bleeps out the bad words. The problem is that I truly believe deep in my heart that the "s" word is a good word. It expresses so much in four little letters. Its impact when spoken from a proper lady like myself is dynamite. Who would expect a senior citizen retired school teacher with a Masters Degree to talk about all this. That's just silly SHIT!

New EFFEN Brand

I have been hearing more about this new "Effen" Brand wherever I go. All I can glean is that there must be some millionaire who came up with this company name, and it has become a household word. I hear it everywhere from parking lots to household items to electronics to cable systems.

The other night, my husband said, "This EFFEN Cable system really sucks. Here we are right at the turning point of the story, and the cable goes out. Now I need to call the "Effen Cable Company so they don't EFFEN bill us for a movie we didn't see."

Yesterday, we were walking to our car in the parking lot, and he said, "I can't believe it. Look at that Effen 4 x 4 parked right next to our Boxster. Can you believe it? What's wrong with these Effen people?" I assume he was speaking about the executives of the Effen company.

This worldwide business is becoming a household word. I heard my friend say mid-sentence on the phone the other night, "Oh no, the Effen dog is barking again." Unless this Effen company breeds purebreds, "Effen" has become a term like "Xerox" which people use every time they talk about making copies. ("Let's just Xerox it," they say.)

Apparently, the company has delved into the "reader" glasses line as well. My husband constantly whines, "Now where are my Effen glasses?"

I find this whole issue Effen weird.

Geeks In India

Do we all appreciate the group of five geeks in India who save our mental health every hour of every day in America? I have often wondered if there is a DUMB AMERICAN UNIVERSITY in Ramanagara where they train people to tell Americans the obvious when they call in a panic from their keyboards.

"You have to help me. I have a report due in ten minutes, and I can't get my mouse to move!" "Oh, thank goodness, I reached you. I just wrote a 50-page section of my doctoral dissertation, and I've lost it. Have you seen it over there?" "Hello, hello. Are you there? Please, help me. This is a case of life and death. I wrote a scathing letter to my lover, and I mistakenly sent it to my husband. Can you get it back for me?"

They must sit over there in some big room howling at us, saying "Look at this one; you won't believe it!" or "This is classic. Let's post it!" or "My three-year-old brother could figure this one out." As one of the "dumb Americans," I don't want to know what they're saying. Just fix the damned problem so I can finish what I'm doing before my hair appointment.

One of the most annoying things about the Indian geeks is their ability to articulate to ONE single timbre. If they pronounce things any more clearly, I'm going to throw my iPhone across the room. They always sound so damned happy. I guess that's how you feel when you are always feeling smarter than the person to whom you are speaking. It must be how husbands feel. (We allow you to feel that way so we can get the remote and the charge card.)

I suppose we should be thankful that with a three-second call, we can get the help we need. It usually doesn't take more than three or four hours to resolve the issue, and now I know the difference between a modem and a motet.

Much Ado About Nothing

I know you are in here somewhere! I just spent 45 minutes writing a wonderful treatise on the fascinating selection of television programming. You were a Pulitzer Prize winning piece, and somehow you just disappeared--Poof! I tried every possible way I know to find you. I "searched," I "right-clicked," I "rebooted," I walked away and came back, I spoke softly to the Dali Lama, but to no avail. Nothing. I checked in the "Recycle" bin, I went through every document I have written for the past three years. Nothing. So, here I am once again--a blank page before me.

So what now? I could write about computers. No, that would raise my blood pressure to dangerous levels in light of the above. I could write about the Dali Lama. Hello, Dali! I could write about how I have always wanted to win a Pulitzer prize, OR, I could write about "nothing."

"Nothing" is a word packed with unspoken meaning. Do you remember asking your kids what happened in school that day? "Nothing." Do you recall asking your three-year-old child or grandchild what he was doing in his room when you didn't hear a sound for five minutes? A tiny voice replies, "Nothing." Do you remember asking your husband what he was thinking about? "Nothing." There is a lot of nothing going on in this world. I personally believe there is a secret code language amongst certain groups of people who KNOW what "nothing" means, but the rest of us will be kept forever ignorant.

Think about songs with the word "nothing." "There is Nothing Like a Dame. . . nothing in this world." (Nothing could be more true.) "Nothing could be finer than a trip to Carolina in the morning." We all know that this is true. Or what about colloquialisms such as "Nothing could be further from the truth." "There is nothing you can do about it." It's amazing how often we use this word and think NOTHING of it! If we break the word down, it becomes NO THING, or NOT HING or NOTHING. The whole thing is absurd, and I have NOTHING more to say about it.

Dot.Coms

The world needs more dot.coms. Yes, it does. I have given serious thought to this issue, and here is a list for the holidays:

i'mlosingmymind.com Our company has just the gifts you need, the advice you're craving, the menus you'll love, unforgettable holiday cards and a super-cheap clean-up squad to clean up the mess. WEBSITE UNDER RECONSTRUCTION. check in 2013.

relativesforsale.com Our company will market unwanted relatives who ruin your holidays. Just upload a photo (one in which they look dumb or ugly), and we will take care of the rest. Maximum limit: 47.5

holidaylighting.com   Stop nagging him. Just call us 24 hours before you want your house lit up for the holidays, and we will be there with bells. Labor free. Our lights only. $73.42 per strand.

dinnerparty.com Perplexed about what to serve that's unique and tasty? Check "unique and tasty" link for holiday ideas. Recipes are free and serve a minimum of 200 guests. (calculator included)

apps.com Whatever app you need, you'll find it here. Asparagusapp, germapp, leavehimapp, petpooapp Special holiday prices apply. Expiration: day before yesterday.

holidayletter.com Our creative writers will customize your holiday letter. We specialize in sarcasm, hyperbole and vulgarity. Call 800-funnyha.

grammygifts.com Lost trying to figure out what to give the grandkids that won't be destroyed or swallowed in the first four minutes? We have it all. Send your signed check with no date and no payee to P.O. Box S.C.A.M. Newark, New Jersey 33042. We guarantee you'll be satisfied or your money back.

regifting.com Got gifts you've never used? We have found fail proof ways to regift whatever you have and the recipient will never know. $10 per idea guaranteed arrival within 36 hours of the holiday. If not completely satisfied with the idea, just deal with it. If you had figured it out, you wouldn't have clicked on this site.

santa.com Santa letters customized and personalized for individuals 68 and up. Leave the creative thinking to us. Upload a vintage photo, and go back to sleep. Send envelope with return address along with check for $26.95 per letter. Bold and CAPS extra.

holidaysex.com Site busy.

Apps Laughs

Now that we have figured out what an "App" is, I have some suggestions for helpful "Apps" for Wives, Mothers and working women Retirees.

WIVES/MOTHERS "Apps":

1. Click on GPS app, and SAVE a "Mom's escape" route.
2. Click on GROCERY LIST, and FORWARD to husband's IPhone.
3. Click on NOTES, and write: "Never Order The Endive Salad" again.
4. Click on PHONE, and SAVE "Loony Bin" under "Favorites."
5. Click on "INVESTMENTS," and proceed to nearest bar.

WORKING WOMEN:

1. Click on RESTAURANTS, and proceed to the one with two for one Cosmos.
2. Click on INVESTMENTS, and consider selling your Mercedes.
3. Click on ITUNES, and download SEAL on the way to the spa.
4. Click on GOOGLE, and SEARCH for "Man Who Occasionally Admits He's Wrong."
5. Click on CAMERA, and take photo of clock at end of workday to use as Wallpaper on home computer.

RETIREES:

1. Find IPhone.
2. Turn On.
3. Find Glasses.
4. Look At Pictures (Icons) On Phone.
5. Click On CAMERA, And Take Photo Of Self With Big Smile.
6. Turn Off, And Take Nap.

What's In An Ad?

If I could pursue another career in my golden years, it would be advertising. I am intrigued by the psychology of what makes people buy various products. In my own experience, there are various methods which have been successful in depleting my secret stash.

I recently read that stores that play classical music inspire people to buy. We have a market where I live that does this beautifully, and I never get out of there for less than $100--$67 of which I don't need. It must be the Noodles Rachmaninov!

The most amazing ads recently are those for couples who would like to improve their sex life by sitting in (separate) bathtubs on top of a mountain looking at the stars. This is only one of the ads whose warnings give a whole new meaning to the term "absurd." If the pleasure lasts for more than four hours, call your physician or dial 911. Wouldn't you love to be the operator getting that call?

Innocent children and their "I want to be my kids' best friend" parents are captive audiences for the toy and video game commercials. If you don't buy your kid the latest "in" toy, be it the Justin Bieber doll or the IPhone #28, you have failed as a parent. As a kid, if Santa didn't bring you one of the "hot items," you were a true "L" (loser). By showing the happy functional family gathered around the

Christmas tree or climbing on a 747, doll and earphones in hand, hopeless materialistic parents are guilt-tripped into providing the "best" for their kids.

And then there's the ad for the leaky water pipes. I never quite thought of my bladder in those terms, and I'm not sure that's refreshing. The bottom line is anything we take for whatever ails us is likely to produce side effects which require more drugs. The drug companies get richer, and we go broke and end up recovering from seven ailments instead of one. I am going to have a party for anyone who is not taking any medication and has all his or her parts. I don't think anyone will show.

Just once, I would like to see an ad for a new model car with a frumpy-looking 65-year-old stepping out of it. The 21-year-old slinky pushed-up models with three-mile legs that step out of these vehicles are just too annoying. In other words, if you want to look like this, then spend $78,493 for this sleek sedan. Or, it would suggest that if you want to be in the same "class" as someone looking like Nicole Kidman, then lease this car for $797.62 a month.

Got Milk? Some genius came up with this creative yet simple ad putting a milk mustache on its models. I still haven't figured out if drinking milk benefits the cows, the farmers or cats. Apparently, there is some MILK organization that wants us to drink the stuff. One advantage of the milk mustache is that it hides the lines over my lips, although the chocolate works best, and I look like a real nerd (albeit, a chocolate nerd).

The ad my husband hates most is for an insurance company which features a woman with very red lipstick. He leaves the room when it airs. The strange thing is, however, that I remember the name of the company--maybe because he hates this ad so much. Hey, whatever works.

You Have Encountered An Expected Error. . .

This message flashes on our computer and television screens at totally inappropriate times. This only happens when I am in the middle of making my final edit of my doctoral dissertation, page 379 out of 380. The message goes on to say that if you click on the wrong key, you will LOSE your entire document. Joy. To click or not to click—this is the dilemma. To live joyously or to slit my wrists if I lose this document, there is the real question.

The "error" message also appears when we are watching a thriller on our "Pay on Demand" channel. Just as the killer is creeping around the shrubs, the cops' sirens wailing in the background, the "error" message appears. People have been known to destroy perfectly lovely HD television screens when this occurs. The good news is that you can call the cable company immediately. They will put you on "hold" (while Neil Diamond sings in the background) with still another message that says, "You will be answered in the order in which this call has been received. You are number 4,372 in the queue." SCREW THE QUEUE! We want to know if the cops arrive in time.

I am waiting for my oven to display this message. If this happens, I would run to my owner's manual (I think it's in the garage under the 1974 paint cans). I would look up "errors" in the manual, and it would read, "When the **unexpected error** sign flashes, be sure to turn off all electricity in the house as the oven will explode within five to ten minutes. It has already taken me 8.7 minutes to find the manual. Oh, my.

There is only ONE unexpected error I should have heeded. That's the one that signaled my brain to get out of bed that day!

Virus

Dear G.S.:

My name is Mini (that's short for MINIscule). To some this may imply that my pain is half what a "mighty" might experience. Not true. I am presently locked up in ICU because a virulent virus has taken over my entire body. You would not believe what I have been through: poking, prodding, tests, more poking, more tests. (I'm about to get loaded!) It's been three days, and I haven't seen the same person twice. I have no clue who is in charge, and I am allowed no visitors. I'm confident that my parents are beside themselves with no way to communicate, not to mention the cost of all this with no insurance. They were going to get me the virus protection injection, but "Oh my, cough cough" got busy and forgot, and "Happy Feet" hasn't a clue when it comes to spending money with no shoes involved. I've been stripped naked, and I am so cold. They leave me alone all night in the dark.

desperate,

hp

Lists

My To Do lists have changed since I retired five years ago. Before I walked out of my classroom, my home of 25 years, a typical list would look like this:

1. Write lesson plans
2. Correct papers
3. Talk to "Jacques" about his oral points
4. Work on grades for 3rd quarter
5. Do laundry
6. Plan dinner party for Saturday
7. Buy groceries
8. Make hair appointment
9. Wash bathroom floor
10. Drop off suits at cleaners

Now, my list looks more like this:

1. Get up
2. Wash face
3. Have breakfast
4. Take vitamins
5. Make bed
6. Read

7. Set alarm to get back up from bed
8. Make bed again
9. Get laundry ready for husband to do
10. Read Facebook

How times have changed.

My First Pension Check

My first pension check. This can't be mine—I'm way too young! My grandparents got pension checks, I get CVS coupon books. My parents have a pension, but they live in Florida. No, there has to be a mistake. I'm way too young for this.

The "A" word ("aging") plagues me daily now. I keep lying to myself telling my "semi-buff" body that it looks better than it did when I was 30. Who am I kidding? Yes, I was heavier then, but my skin didn't crackle.

I have to admit the AARP magazine has some dynamite articles although I have to take out my contacts to read them. I highly resent, however, the stars they flaunt on the covers. Why don't they put someone on there that really LOOKS their age and write about how they're dealing with it (like moi, par exemple!)

Some Sadist started putting pictures in the obituaries. Now I find myself reading them, paying close attention to the ages of the deceased. I'm glad to say that the pictures of most of them are about 25 years old.

Conversations with our friends are changing. I will not participate in the following topics yet, however: cholesterol, colonoscopies, long-term care insurance, diets, senior discounts or grandchildren's first words. Always trying to steer the conversation toward something uplifting like the latest mystery I've read or the first dessert I've made since 1964. No talk about doctors unless they're GQ–worthy.

À MARAT.

DAVID.

Celebrity Letters

Dear Mom and Dad:

I am here at camp in the woods with my friends. I am listening to the bells tolling while rubbing my arms that are tired from lugging my backpack around for two weeks. I am getting ready to say "FAREWELL" to them! We're supposed to be having an "Immovable Feast" soon, whatever that is. If it's "immovable," how are we supposed to eat it? The sun is also rising, as I write, so I'd best get moving. When can I come home?

Love,
Ernest

Dear Mom and Dad:

I am here at camp trying to block out the babble from these tall people wearing crested shirts trying to boss us little guys around. They are obviously egomaniacs without my MENSA mentality. If you ask me, it's all bullshit! When can I come home?

Yours,
George

Dear Mom:

I am here at summer camp with a bunch of other girls my age. We are all fat, but we were told yesterday that there's some spa in Chicago where we can go to lose all of this baby fat. Chicago. Wouldn't that be great? I could go there, get skinny like the Barbie doll, get famous and give things away. What a dream! In the meantime, I am sharing my toys and my socks with my new friends. Don't forget to come get me tomorrow.

Love,
O

Dear Dad:

I hope you and Mom are fine. I haven't heard from you for several days, and I'm not sure what I'm supposed to do next. The camp is fun, but I get bored sometimes. I'm trying to decide whether to go on a hike today or to go swimming with my new camper friends. What do you think I should do? It's hard making decisions. Also, one of my pals has smuggled in some beer, and he wants me to drink some with him. I am afraid that once I start, I won't be able to stop. (Isn't that true?) Write soon, Dad, and say hi to Mom and my brother.

Love,
George

Dear Mom and Dad:

I am here at camp, and I'm getting all kinds of scary ideas for my composition class. Third grade is supposed to be hard, so I thought I would start getting ready early. There is a haunted car here that I've named Christine. It's so cool. I am also studying the dictionary to find cool vocabulary that no one else would think of. Some day, I will become a great writer, and people will make movies out of my books. I told that to one of my pals here, and he just laughed in my face. I decked him. I would rather work on my writing than go on nature hikes with these simpletons, but what can you do? Thanks for sending me to camp. I know you must be missing me a lot.

Stephen

Dear Mom and Dad:

I have been talking to a lot of my camper pals here in the mountains. Each of them comes from somewhere else, and there are a lot of rich ones here. I ask them lots of questions, and I find them all fascinating. Each one's story is different, and I have asked myself if any of them could be famous one day. I am writing down all their answers so that I can tell you about them when I come home. Don't feel you have to rush here to get me. I'm fine, and I'm having lots of fun.

Love,
Larry

Dear Mom and Dad:

What the hell were you thinking sending me to this pit? I am dying here. Everyone is so cheerful, it's making me sick. I hate camping. We were out in the woods last night, and it poured rain all over our tent. It fell in on me just as I was getting out to go to the outhouse. Is there some reason you are putting me through this? I was not born with a silver spoon in my mouth to do grunt work and make crafts with a bunch of lowlifes. I want to come home NOW. Please advise.

Your daughter in anger,

Me

Dear Butch:

You may not remember me, but I was your sister in 1958. I used to cry on your furry head on the back steps. Remember? Where are you now? I am sending this to "Spaniel Heaven" assuming that you are there. How are things there? Are you getting enough of those biscuits Daddy used to give you when you sat up, rolled over, jumped up and down on your hind legs and spoke Spanish? I had to do that too, but he wouldn't even let me go out with boys until I was 24. You were obviously the favorite.

I remember you had such a sweet little taffy face. You had sad eyes, but there was a glint of mischief in them as though you really had the old man figured out. I wonder if it was you who lifted his gold watch and buried it somewhere. He looked for it for years. It was YOU, wasn't it? That was how you got back at him for making you feel like a circus clown.

Remember how you weren't allowed to go in the living room? I wasn't either! Didn't you just want to sneak in there and pee all over Mom's designer couch? I did! (want to, that is). I did sneak in there when she wasn't home and got felt up by my 8th grade boyfriend. I wonder what ever happened to him. He was so cute.

Remember how my sister tried to ride you like a horse? She was whacked. She still is, 60 years later. She used to get on your back and flatten you to the floor. You were such a good sport about it. Didn't you just want to bite her friggin' nose off? I have wanted to do that for years, but I was taught to vent in other ways. (We won't go there).

Do you have a girlfriend up there, Butch? I hope so, as I don't want you to be lonely. Do they give you chores like licking the pearly gates? I can't imagine what it's like there. Are there only Spaniels or do they let in a stray lab or pug when you're not looking? Is there a set of "house rules?"

Well, I know you can't write, Butch, but please know I think of you often, and I will never forget the comfort you gave me when I blew my nose in your fur!

Love,
Sis

Letters To My Husband

Dear Honey:

I love you so much. You are sweet and kind and always there when I need you.

Would you please take out the garbage and hang our new painting. (the one I bought when you weren't looking.)

Dear Honey:

I feel so blessed that we have had so much time together. I'll bet you could use some time to yourself.

Dear Honey:

Yesterday when you called me bad names, I know it's just because you saw the five bags in my closet. Now that you're already upset, I will bring in the rest of them.

Dear Honey:

The kids really miss you. Go ahead and take a few days to drive 13 hours to see them.

Dear Honey:

I know you want to move to Florida. I realize it gets very cold and gray here. You go for it, honey, and write soon.

Dear Honey:

Thanks for letting me drink last night. I had a wonderful time! What's your name again?

Dear Honey:

I am very grateful that you do all the laundry. If you want to add the cooking to the list, I won't stand in your way.

Dear Honey:

I won't nag you about anything ever again if you pay me what you owe me for 20 years of cooking your meals, organizing our social life, planning our trips, birthing your children and providing you with a three million dollar pension.

Letter To My Drama Teacher

Dear Mrs. Milne:

I am sending you this letter way up there in acting heaven. I know you are happy in your element, and I want to thank you for planting the drama seed in my brain and heart early in my life.

Before I was in your sixth grade "Auditorium" class (no one knew that there was subject matter associated with the stage in those days), I didn't realize the talent that was growing within me. YOU and the doors you opened for me are responsible, at least in part, for my now being a drama queen.

I can provide drama anywhere I go. You unleashed some channel of creative energy in me in 1953, and it's still rushing out of my pores one hundred years later. I can cry on demand, scream without much provocation, pout anytime, anywhere, embellish and exaggerate at the drop of a drawer, and I have actually been paid to do all of these things ON A STAGE.

As you look down from the wings (or are you wearing them?), I hope you are smiling fondly at my daily life of drama and comedy.

You are watching a script in the making, and I promise to send you at least 6% of the royalties when they call me to L.A. I even have a schtick for the TSA screeners ready.

Yours very truly,
Sandy

Letters To My Shrinks

Dear Shrinks of the past 20 years:

I am just fine, thankyouverymuch. Y'all helped me see the light when I was in the dark. Y'all always helped me see that it was never MY fault. Y'all helped me learn how to take care of myself first. Y'all reminded me to ask myself your favorite questions:

1. How's that workin' for ya?
2. How do ya feel about that?
3. What do ya think that says to ya?
4. How else could you frame that?
5. How else could you have handled that?

What the......? I paid y'all $73,296.33 for five questions my neighbor's retarded six-year-old could have come up with.

Y'all have helped me to become the well-rounded, ecstatically happy quintessential NARCISSIST that I am today.

Thanks from the bottom of my savings account.

Fifi

The Holiday Letter

Yes, I admit it. I cannot lie. I send a holiday letter. Is it clever and cute? Of course. Is it informative and entertaining? You betcha.

Some people should never write a holiday letter, however. I am begging you to just give it up. Go watch your favorite sitcom on the couch with your Doritos and beer and forget about it. You would be doing your friends and relatives a major favor.

Below, you will find an example of the forbidden Holiday letter writer.

Dear family&frenz:

just hangin' out this year. not much happenin' The kids are going to school. thats a good thing. wish they'd stay there longer tho. Joe's still workin', and thats a goodthing. they cut his overthyme, so he's spending more time with his Millers on the couch. that's never gonna change, so i don't know why i'm even talkin' about it. the man was born with a football in his mouth, i swear.

i'm doin' good. work is goin' ok, and i sneak some texting in when no one's looking. you can't smoke at work anymore tho, so i have to wait till i get in the truck.

the kids have there activities so i run them all over hell everyday. if it's not soccer, it's football practice or ballet lessons. who knew a Pleeyay would cost half a paycheck a month?

the dog is good. he's got a new friend down the street, so he's happy. i don't like walking him when he sees her tho. it takes much longer for the walk, if you know what i mean.

my throat is sore after the Tea Party rally last week, but I take los-sangeles and that sooze me.

well, enjoy the photos i sent. i couldn't get anymore on the page. hope you can tell me from the dog.

love to y'all

joyce & brood

I Want A Divorce

I can't take it anymore. Not one more day with you. I've tried everything, and nothing works. Therapy? Are you even kidding? There's
no therapy that will solve this problem.

A week-end retreat? What good will that do? I will still have to look
in the mirror when I get home. And what will I see? The same OLD
face. Yes, the same one. The one who won't compromise, won't let
go of the ego, won't accept. It's time. I want a divorce. I am leaving
you. YOU, my OLD FACE.

Before filing:

Every morning I get up, and you just don't go away. There are little
scratches here and there. I don't wear my rings or my watch, so
unless there is some insect alien invading my pillow, Mother Nature
is being a real wench!

Then there are tiny little red puffs at the top of my cheekbones.
How can they be there? It's not like I am balancing on the frame of
my face all night.

The worst part though is the mouth area. Above my lips, there are a
million little lines like ski runs which go from the bottom of my nose

to my top lip. Under the bottom lip, there appears to be a mogul or two. Try running your lip stain over those puppies. My smile is headed south. It's not that I don't laugh all day because I do. I see much humor in the world around me, and I celebrate it hourly. The problem is that when I smile, my lips go down instead of up. I am going to have to stand on my head soon so people will know I am not sad. That adds a whole new dimension to my sexy wardrobe.

The jowls have been trying to make their own statement for over a year. They apparently need attention because they are all puffed up like they've been bragging. I just want to get some duct tape and push those little buggers down.

We won't even go there with the neck. Even after $10,000 surgery, if I turn my head, the folds are still visible. At least, I don't have to wear turtlenecks anymore to look like a human being.

Is 70 the new 67? I'm hanging on with all my Retin-A!

Flawless Skin? I Hate You

If you are over 60 and have great skin, I hate you. I hate you, your mother, your grandmother and your Aunt Gretchen. You have good skin genes. Why did you get them, and I didn't? Fine, I got great legs, good toe nails and fab elbows, but YOU—you got the beautiful smooth, flawless skin. I hate you.

Tonight, I noticed that my midriff, even though it is toned and six-packed, is wrinkling as I write. This may be the last year of the two-piece for yours truly. At 67, I guess I should be thankful that I've made it this far with a smooth torso. I am angry, however, as I hoped to get to the big seven zero in my bikini. Guess not. It could be worse. I could have a muffin top like many of my friends. They don't pay hundreds of dollars per month, though, for an in-home trainer and hours of lifting 400-pound weights over my teeth. (If I don't drop one of those puppies on my cuspids, it is going to be a miracle.)

We were at a dinner party tonight. The average age was 84. I looked around, and I thought to myself, "Wow, you look pretty good, girl-friend." Then I sat down across from two 50-somethings whose skin looked like they'd never spent one second in the sun. I hated them instantly. One was chubby, so she didn't count. I have figured out that if you're at least 40 pounds overweight, the skin will remain taut over the fat, and it will look good even if it's thin and old. The other one is a size quadruple zero, and she had the gall to be pretty too. I told myself she was probably 46, but I think she was about 57. The nerve.

I wish I had noticed my mother's skin and my grandmothers' skin. In those days, I wasn't paying attention to skin. If I had paid attention, I would have known whether my days are numbered before I am a total prune. I was too busy chasing men and trying to be a size quadruple zero to worry about skin. To me, lying in the sun for hours with baby oil plastered all over my body was much more fun than worrying about what I'd look like when I got old (like now).

Now that I have done things to my face, I notice everyone's face-- even the fertilizer guy's. Where are the wrinkles? Are there sink holes in the lower cheeks? (the ones on the face) Does the nose look like it's got railroad tracks down the bridge? Do the eyelids look like they are trying to protect the irises like eye-awnings? Do the puckers around the mouth look like I'm holding marbles in them? Oh, my. Such scrutiny. Such sadness.

You cannot be my friend unless you understand all of this, and if you have perfect skin, don't even talk to me.

Where Does The Makeup Go?

Every morning, I put on my makeup before I begin my day out in the world. I carefully paint my face to hide every wrinkle, brown spot and blemish. I feel sorry for men who don't have this luxury (at least not in our circles).

At the end of the day, I take my make-up exfoliator wipe (a minuscule hanky with little bumps all over it to take half the skin off your face) and wipe my face. Nothing. There is absolutely nothing on the little cloth. Where did it go? Where did the foundation, the blush, the mascara, the eye shadow go? How can there be enough room in my pores for 50 years worth of all that? If it left the pores after disappearing from my face, then where is it now? Is it in my sinuses, behind my eye sockets, under my gums, embedded in my ear wax? Yuck. For the price I pay for this make-up, I could take a trip to Europe every six months. If it is disappearing everyday, then I am absorbing hundreds of dollars into my blood stream, and I can't even cash in on it. There's something wrong here.

I'll bet the nice lady at the makeup counter knows where it goes. She's all smiles when she wants me to buy $475-worth of her products, but I'll bet she's laughing up her sleeve because she knows all that money is in my body somewhere, absorbed by greedy pores and sweat glands.

In my next life, I won't need make-up, as I will be so naturally beautiful that I won't need any enhancing. Enhancing, huh! My makeup doesn't enhance, it HIDES many sins. Each day I wake up with a new one. This morning I looked in the mirror to discover a cut on my nose and a big red splotch next to my left eye. Either someone beat me up while I was sleeping, or the make-up is trying to find its way out, and these are the stretch marks.

I just realized that the word MAKEUP tells it all. It is a way to make up for what the Big Guy didn't give us. A "make-up" match in tennis is a DO OVER. A "make-up" test is a TRY AGAIN. Or maybe it means, let's make up a better face than the one you've got there, sister.

This is all making me tired.

Looking Down On Me

If I were up in a plane looking down at myself, it would make for a great slapstick comedy. I have imagined watching myself doing the following:

Trying to pluck my eyebrows when I can barely see my eyes.
Trying to get the cover off a new CD.
Counting the seconds between my husband's snores.
Putting my wicked big toenail through my new pair of hose.
Trying to get out of a tight sweater at a ritzy boutique without calling for help.
Trying not to look embarrassed after spilling my wine all over the hostess's new tablecloth.
Trying to close the door of the gas tank on my new car without looking like an idiot.
Smiling at the driver I just cut off.
Looking confident after losing my tennis match 6-0.
Trying to open a package of cheese.
Trying to act cool after my grandchild bit me and screamed hysterically at McDonald's.
Trying to get my credit card out of my two front teeth while attempting to extract a piece of spinach.
Throwing a tantrum.
Trying not to slap my mother-in-law when she insults me.

Hugging my stuffed bear.

Counting my brown spots.

Thinking creatively when finding there's no toilet paper in the restaurant bathroom.

Shoes Have Voices

"RIGHT HERE! YOU MUST TRY ME!" "NO, OVER HERE. THESE ARE TOTALLY YOU!" "ARE YOU EVEN KIDDING? WE ARE MADE FOR YOU, AND WE'RE 50% OFF!"

I have tried everything to block out the voices, but nothing works. I put my iPod earbuds in my ears as deep as they will go without bruising my brain. I have stayed out of the stores, but then the coupons come in my e-mail. I have tried walking right by the shoe sales, and some force of nature just sucks my body right through the double doors and into the shoe department.

People make fun of me because they think I have so many pairs of shoes. Actually, most of my friends have many more pairs than me. Mine are just taller and more "out there." Bows, zippers, cuffs, flowers, feathers—all MOI! My friend told me at the store this morning that she is going to have the Alzheimer's test. Why would I do that to myself?" I said. I want to remember what's on these feet as long as possible, and when I can't remember, I will assign the job to one of the day nurses.

I figure I've got another five years left in me to balance in my stilettos so I need to stock up and step out as often as possible before it's too late. After the five years, I may have to move down into wedgies and flats. This will be doubly bad, as I will have shrunk by then, so instead of looking 5'8", I will be 4'6". Not good.

I also have to worry that there may be a shortage of leather one day, and I want to be prepared. Look at what's happened to polyester and silk shantung!

I have begun putting lotion on my feet because I've been dancing, climbing, stomping, running, jumping, tiptoeing and sliding on them for years. I must take care of them. Maybe soon they will have sole implants!

Crabby Cuspids

It's no wonder dentists have the highest suicide rate. If I had to look at what they do every day of my life, I would definitely look for a quick escape. It's the hygienists; however, who annoy me the most, mainly because they are always so cheerful.

I would be cheerful too if I could put a mask on my face at 8:00 a.m., sit on a stool, take out my aggression on someone's gums with a tiny orange-caramel-flavored jack hammer and spit out my life story to my captive audience. The poor fool in the chair can't interrupt, and even if he wanted to make a comment, he'd have to get the suck tube out of his mouth and wipe off his entire face before responding. And that's assuming he could remember his comment by then.

In my experience, most hygienists are women. My theory is that their husbands don't or won't listen to them, so they use us, the clients, as their listening posts. I know the life histories of every hygienist who has ever flossed my molars. I know their kids' names, what colleges they attended, what honors they earned, how much their parents paid for their educations and where they are now. Just in case, I forget any of those details, I am sure to get an update at my next six-month checkup.

In dental school, they must teach these women some chair-side manners because they always ask me questions about my family and my life. The rub is that I can't respond (and they know that), so I spit, "Oh, zehrfinethanyo." Let's face it, all these women care about is grinding and scraping every last speck of plaque off whatever is left of our cuspids so the dentist won't yell at them. I'd like to take their little picks and scrapers and scratch their front teeth with hazlenut-flavored tar!

Feet

When I was very young, I had beautiful feet. They were perfectly formed with straight toes, lovely nails and no blemishes. Fifty years and over 1000 pairs of stilettos later, my toes are out of control, and my feet are powerless.

My stepmother has toes that extend outside of her peep-toe old-lady sandals and wrap around the soul of her shoes. Three of the toes on each foot veer off to the left or right and are vulnerable to traffic. The big toes curl up at the ends, and the baby toes are totally deformed. She tells me that this is what I have to look forward to because I have abused my appendages for so long. Joy. I remember my mother saying, "The day I can't wear my heels, just hoist me into the box!" I remember laughing at that, but now it isn't so funny.

As this topic has been on my mind of late (waking me up in the middle of the night), I unconsciously found myself examining my friends' toes. Having gone on a short trip with 11 other women my age, I was amazed and comforted to find deformity is the norm. Whew! If I have to have custom-made stilettos made in my 80s, I will have lots of company. Interestingly enough, none of these women wore or wear high heels, and their toes are still deformed!

I figure it's too late to change my ways now. I like it up here. The taller my heels, the thinner I look. Once I take them off, I will have to immediately shed ten pounds. I can eat more up here, feel more powerful and in control up here and see the dust on your refrigerator top up here. Life is good up high. It is obvious that I will pay a price one day soon, but until then, I will enjoy the tall air.

Celebrate Your Nose

I declare this month "Celebrate your Nose" month! Yes, get out there folks and flaunt that nose—hold it high. Be proud and grateful for your sinuses! Breathe in, breathe out. Wiggle it around. Scrunch it up! Rub it. Pet it. Squeeze it. If it doesn't meet your demands, PICKIT!

Noses come in all shapes and sizes, packaged in everything from freckles to zits. Some even come equipped with little hairs inside that when bored, one can comb. This month, everywhere you go, observe the nose. See where it's aimed. See how its owners treat it. Do the measure-it-in-your-mind thing. Compare it to others you see and to your own. Does it dominate the person's face, or does it look like a heavenly afterthought. Are people blowing it, scratching it, looking at it, sniffing with it?

Think of how we take the nose for granted. How many nights before bed do you get on your knees and thank some heavenly power for your proboscis? Have you ever thought about where you'd be without it? For example, how could you grimace at yucky grandma casseroles without it? How could you wear your favorite Martian glasses without it? What would happen to the "Puff" company? People would lose jobs. What would happen to inhaler manufacturers?

How would you get into other peoples' business? What would hold your two eyes apart? I'll bet you never thought about all this.

Without the nose, we would all have to breathe through our mouths. Millions of citizens would walk the streets with their mouths open. Insects could get in there, not to mention sawdust and bird droppings. People in dry climates would suffer from the shrivel-tongue disease, and they wouldn't be able to talk. All desert states would no longer have a voice. There would be a major drain on the water supply there, and the Colorado River is already getting time and a half. Air fresheners would disappear along with all the wick-workers.

Smell would be a luxury of the past. No cinnamon toast wafting out of the toaster. No lilacs welcoming spring. No fresh-baked apple pie greeting you as you enter grandma's kitchen. No newly-mowed grass to remind you it's summer. No scent of a woman. No bad breath. No need for Listerine and Scope or its work force. On the other hand, flatulence would lose its bad name.

So, indulge yourself in the value of your nose this month. Celebrate its prominence on your face. Caress it for all it offers you day after day. Point it out to a stranger. Let's promote Nose Awareness. Take a picture of it and post it on your calendar. Laugh at it. Thank it. Take a deep breath in, and exhale. Now be glad you can breathe so you can live long enough to celebrate another part of your magnificent body.

Dear Girl Scouts of America, Inc.

I am holding you personally responsible for my eating disorder. I got over the pecan sandie binging. I have survived the ice cream crisis and I'm still working on the wine war, but Girl Scout cookies. What loyal American citizen can resist the mint patties or the chocolate peanut butter melt-in-your-mouths? It's just not fair.

It all started when I was 11. My grandpa died, and I was not allowed to go to his funeral. I barely knew him, but that was beside the point. All I could do with my distraught little mouth was to lock myself in the closet with a box (not a couple), a box of Girl Scout wafers. That was the beginning of a lifetime of binging on sweets, and it's all your fault! There should have been a warning to mothers: "Mothers: any daughters who indulge in these goodies will NOT enjoy a Twiggy body---EVER!" I never saw my mother or my father sitting Indian style in the closet indulging in the GS conspiracy. I must have had a chemical imbalance.

It has been over 50 years since that fateful day when I climbed out of the closet 10 pounds heavier than when I went in! I no longer binge on cookies because I went to Girl Scout therapy and had hypnosis to rid myself of the uncontrollable urge to gorge myself to support the badge charity.

You should be ashamed.

P.S.   If you would like to make this up to me, you can send me a coupon for a year's session with a personal trainer. I have one in mind. I think he's Governor of California.

Dear Mr. Dunkin':

What were you thinking? Do you realize that 60% of our country is overweight, and 59% of them said their favorite food was the DONUT? YOUR donuts!?? If I could pig out on any food that would not make me fat or sick, I would rush right over to your establishment, climb over the counter, pass the fab DD coffee, grab three pink and white boxes and fill them with glazed sticks! How does that make you feel? If I told you that I was 63, 4'9" and 189 pounds in my bare feet, would you feel any different? I was 42, 5'6" and 132 in those days.

They used to call me "donuts." That was not because I overdosed on carrot sticks! Your donuts are sinful. They should come with little notes of confession to take to the booth so that the priest would know exactly how many Hail Marys to recommend. The little notes would probably have the aroma of your kitchen on them though, and the priest himself would most likely make a mad dash to your store. Talk about SHAME—it's YOU who ought to feel shame bringing all this pleasure to the world. So many donuts, so little time.

I figure that throughout my life, I have had at least 2400 donuts. I don't even want to think about the calories I've ingested, much less the sugar. I am sure my dentist loved you, and my students couldn't wait to see me coming with the big box.

And then, you weren't satisfied selling us the positive space, you had to market the negative space too—the HOLE. All that is a teaser to make you go back to buy the rest. Very clever indeed.

Well, I am cured. The thought of all of that sugar on my tongue repulses me anymore. I can't do it. I am now 5'6", and I weigh a lithe 124 pounds. No glaze, filling or frosting can tempt me. Thanks for the ride, but I've landed, and I choose NOT to be a statistic.

Stress-Free Diet Regimen

Breakfast: 4 anti-depressants
                Lunch: Nap
Dinner: 1/2 bottle of red wine

Breakfast: one piece of dry toast
Lunch: 1/4 oz. of tuna
Dinner: 5 sleeping pills

Breakfast: one soft-boiled egg
Lunch: one lettuce salad with no dressing
Dinner: 4 oz. cooked salmon
Midnight: 3 chocolate candy bars

Breakfast: One cup of strong black coffee
Lunch: Two oranges
Dinner: 8 oz. asparagus
Midnight: 1/2 gallon Caramel Delight ice cream

Breakfast: one slice wheat bread toasted with one oz. cheese on top
Lunch: one slice wheat bread with 2 oz. turkey on top
Dinner: one husband in bed with him on top

Breakfast: one energy bar before six-mile run
Lunch: one glass of whey protein chocolate shake after 45-minute resistance workout
Dinner: one vodka tonic before yoga workout

Breakfast: one morning delight
Lunch: one afternoon delight
Dinner: 5 scoops Edy's Caramel Delight

Breakfast: one valium
Lunch: two valium
Dinner: three sleeping pills

Breakfast: one winning lottery ticket
Lunch: one Publishers' Clearing House check
Dinner: one free Porsche

Breakfast: guess
Lunch: imagine
Dinner: fill in the blank

Dear Mr. House:

You don't know me, but I've been enjoying your product for years! When I was first introduced to you, Maxwell, I thought to myself, "What a sophisticated name!" Since that time, I have been so high on your caffeine that I really don't care what your name is. Just keep making that stuff!

One little cup of your intoxicating liquid can have multiple effects on me. First of all, it makes me very creative. The juices just flow and flow. I owe it to you that my lesson plans of 40 years were the zaniest in the land. Secondly, I become extremely animated, and that has kept my students awake all those years. Many begged me not to talk first and second hours, but I ignored them and inspired them into oblivion. Finally, the caffeine has kept me lithe because I don't eat. When you're shaking from the narcotic effects of the liquid, it is difficult to think of cramming gobs of pasta and sausage in the pie hole. I just let the black stuff do its thing.

You know, Max, I feel like we have really bonded over the years. You must be a millionaire by now, and I admire that about you. When I am wide awake at 3 a.m. writing my memoirs, I think of you. My writing is "good to the very last drop."

Great Minds Collide

Imagine what fascinating literary masterpieces could have been produced had some of the greatest   minds of our century collaborated on their novels. Here are a few I would have put on my bookshelf:

The French Lieutenant's Mockingbird

A Long Day's Journey into Winesburg, Ohio

The Old Man and the Little Women

The Sound East of Eden

Uncle Tom's Treasure

Of Mice and Lady Chatterly

Women in the Wind

A Separate Wrath (Sour Grapes)

Huckleberry X

Portnoy's Cold Blood

The Scarlet Salesman

Catcher in the Slaughterhouse

Man's Search for Madame Bovary

Invisible Moby

Native Zelda

A Farewell to Prince

Wrath and Fury

Guess Who's Coming to Cannery Row: The Little Dick

The Queery Letter

Dear Mr. Smithe:

"Laughter is the best medicine." I don't know who said that but they were write. Laughing is good, and when you read my book, you will see right away that I really really like to write. I like to laugh sometimes too.

My book doesn't follow any real logical format. It's just a random bunch of short snippets about life scene from a humorous perspective.

They're several pieces about the human body that I think you'll find funny. My girlfriend, Nancy, really liked them, and she doesn't think ANYTHING is funny. My shrink liked some of the chapters about technology, as she doesn't know much about it.

I am qualified to right this book because I have a grate cents of humor. I laugh at almost everything. I am educated to. I have a BA in Framing and 28 hours past it in paranormal psychology

I hope yule consider publishing my book. It will bring you're company alot of money.

Sincerely,

Fifi Bomberry

Dear Writer's Block:

You think you're so smart, don't you? You think I don't know what you're trying to do. I get it. I totally understand that you don't want me to succeed. You have a whole recipe of junk to fill up my brain so I can't think. You start with a batter of trivia and banal drivel. Add to that three cups of doubt, a pinch of energy, 10 ounces of drive, two tablespoons of confusion and you whisk it all together with anxiety and frustration. Well, I've got your number. I know what you are trying to do and why. You can't fool me. I will consume this recipe, digest it thoroughly and write the best American novel of the century. Just watch me.

Writing a Short Story for a Writing Competition

Four days to come up with a great winning story of 1500 words or less. What are they thinking? I will have to embellish with asides, parentheses, wonderful alliterative descriptions. . . I don't know if I can do it. Yes, I can. Yes, I can. How many words is that? That's 49 words already, but I don't know if you're supposed to count 1500 as one word or four or if you're supposed to count the punctuation too. Oh, my. This is really hard.

The rules say you have to double space, but does that mean you have to count each line that you haven't typed as however many words would have been in it? And do you have to count the title words too?

The first step is coming up with a topic and title which will catch the judge's attention. "Writing a Short Story for a Writing Competition" just may not cut it. It needs to "grab" the reader. "Writing a Short Story While Hung over" might work or "Hung over At A Writing Competition," "Short Hangovers Make Good Stories," or "Hangover

Competing Makes Great Short Stories." As I don't drink, this will not work.

I'm now at 240 words, and I haven't even said anything. It took me seven minutes to do the math. (I hated my third grade teacher.)

Writing short stories is difficult for those of us who have so much to say and so little time left. We have infinite amounts of wisdom to share and doggerel to send the reader right over the edge. The word "short" is not one that I embrace on any level. I am not short. I don't speak in short sentences. I don't think in short spurts. I don't marry short men. I don't take short showers or short cuts. I don't even read short stories. If the book isn't at least 4500 pages long, I am not interested. How can I ask myself to compose a "short" story? That's the long and short of it.

I just left the computer to research the secrets of winning a "Short" story contest in my Writer's Digest manuals. It didn't help much, as I have a very "short" attention span, and I am on a time crunch now with only three days and several hours left to finish this award-winning puppy.

Maybe I need a "short" nap. Yes, that's it. It will refresh my creative thinking.

OK. I think that helped. That was the "shortest" nap I ever took. I feel a new rush of energy now. I am ready to work feverishly to create the most memorable piece of "short" fiction ever imagined.

Once upon a time, there was a short story. He was very jealous of the tall story because passers-by would look up at the tall story and admire its gleaming windows which reflected the skyline and flowing river. The short story reflected nothing more than the bag ladies whose heads were buried in the garbage cans in front of the building. Short Story could do nothing about his fate; he was what he was, and there was no room for growth or self-pity. Maybe if he paid a visit to Tall Story, he could get some advice.

"Mr. Tall Story," he said speaking loudly so as to be heard 137 flights up. "I really wish I could be a tall story. How can I grow tall and strong like you?"

"Sorry, Short Story," he smiled down. "We must accept what the architects have given us. Once you're built, there's no room for modification. You just have to be the best Short Story you can be. Try to think of a way to gain attention and fame just being what you are."

Short Story was disheartened. He could not think of one thing he could do to be as elegant and admired as his neighbor. He decided to take a short nap. When we awoke, it came to him. Short spurts of energy and creative ideas flashed before his eyes, and in a very short time, he came up with the answer: A Baseball Café in front of his building called "Short Stop" would bring him instant fame. He called the local Baseball Commission and pitched his story. They loved it, and six months later, a bustling "SHORT STOP" drew fans from all over town. There were flat screen televisions attached to baseball bat stands for fans to watch the game of the moment while drinking

"Short" beers and eating "Short" ribs. There were also "Short" chops, "Short Shots" and "Short" cake on the six-inch menu.

The local newspapers and television stations loved the concept. They arrived in droves to do a "short" story on the "Short Stop," and it was aired for a short time until people had to be turned away for lack of table space.

Eight hundred seventy words. Almost there. In a short time, cynics began to chant, "It won't last; it's the trend of the moment. Soon, the café will close, and they'll have to short sale the place. Trendy places always come up short." Short Story resented the doubters. They had short-term vision. Short Story put on his thinking cap once again, imagining a new gimmick to bring in customers. His new ads were brilliant: "You'll be Short of Breath when you taste our new "Short Stack" breakfasts served with one free ticket to the Mets game." "Try our "Short Cuts" beef-kabobs, shish-kabobs, Thingamabobs. A free baseball signed by Alex Rodriguez (famous for his own brand of "short cuts.") "For you seniors out there, try our brand new "short-wasted" drink served in a crystal baseball.

After launching an aggressive marketing campaign, business flour-ished, and Short Story had to turn away reservations. In less than a year, the business did more than 2.5 million dollars. Shortly after he began selling "pitchers" of beer served by "Bat Girls," Oprah invited him to appear on her show. Flattered by her offer, Short Story accepted, with the caveat that her crew would obviously have to come to him. A short time later, Oprah and her entourage sat in the "Pitchers Box," the best table in the house. "OK, "Short Stuff," she winked, "just how did you take one short story and turn it into a 2.5 million dollar business?" Short Story stopped short and replied, "To make a long story short, I got all wound up, and I pitched short. It was a home run."

This makes 1164 words. As this is the "short" version, I certainly hope the judges will be relieved (a relief pitch).

Acknowledgments

The most obvious person to thank for inspiring me to write this book is my late father, Chet Bloomquist. He was my cheerleader, my mentor, my soul mate and my best friend for years and years. He was silly, master of the pun, creative, funny and full of life until the end of his 92 years. He loved my writing when my professors weren't so sure, and he always encouraged me to take a risk. He believed that every experience, good or bad, was one from which to learn and grow. Thank you, Daddy.

My husband replaced my father 18 years ago as my soul mate and best friend. He has patiently read and laughed at some of my most absurd work. His encouragement and love have inspired me to follow my passion, and he has been a wonderful sport being the target of some of my ruthless humor. Thank you, Mark.

My coach, Alice Osborn, has stood by me for counseling and encouraging my efforts. Her edits are sound and useful, and I respect her opinion and appreciate her guidance on my writing journey.

My Girls Night Out Group has been wonderful giving me feedback and support as I write day after day. Much of what we talk about together finds its way into my prose. Thank you Marion Hawkins,

Beth Van Amberg and Claire Mains for being such cherished friends and loyal supporters.

I am proud to say that both of my daughters are excellent writers, and their love sustains me and buoys me every day. I love you, Chris and Kate.

Special thanks go to Dover Publishing for allowing me to use the original classical art in my book.

Reader Survey

Your sincere answers to the following questions will be greatly appreciated.

1. This book was very funny.   Yes____   No____
2. This book was stupid.   Yes____   No____
3. This author should write more.   Yes____   No____

Made in the USA
Charleston, SC
10 June 2011